Words That Listen

A Literary Companion to the Lectionary

Volume 1
Advent to Ascension

Editors
J. Barney Hawkins IV and Ian S. Markham

Consulting Editor
Mark Oakley

Associate Editors
Frank T. Griswold III, Cynthia Briggs Kittredge

Assistant Editor
Gregory L. Millikin

CANTERBURY
PRESS
Norwich

© J. Barney Hawkins IV and Ian S. Markham 2018

First published in 2018 by the Canterbury Press Norwich
Editorial office
3rd Floor, Invicta House
108–114 Golden Lane
London EC1Y 0TG, UK
www.canterburypress.co.uk

Canterbury Press is an imprint of Hymns Ancient & Modern Ltd
(a registered charity)

Hymns Ancient & Modern® is a registered trademark of
Hymns Ancient & Modern Ltd
13A Hellesdon Park Road, Norwich,
Norfolk NR6 5DR, UK

Published in the United States in 2018 by Church Publishing

British Library Cataloguing in Publication data

A catalogue record for this book is available
from the British Library

978 1 78622 064 6

Printed and bound in Great Britain by
CPI Group (UK) Ltd

CONTENTS

Volume 1

INTRODUCTION

The Word of God which we encounter in Holy Scripture is the inspiration for *Words That Listen: A Literary Companion to the Lectionary*. More specifically, these two volumes are made up of literary and artistic selections which "listen" to the gospel readings of the three-year lectionary of the Episcopal Church. In a short poem, Wendell Berry seems to expand the inspired canon and makes a claim for an "incarnate Word" which is "everything that is."

> The incarnate Word is with us,
> is still speaking, is present
> always, yet leaves no sign
> but everything that is.
> (Wendell Berry, "Sabbath IX, 1999")

The Episcopal Church follows an authorized lectionary for readings from the Christian Bible in its worship services. The lectionary is shaped by the church year and, in the course of three years, exposes the faithful to much of the Old Testament and the New Testament. The lectionary means that the presider or preacher is not free to pick a reading which is on their mind or which seems appropriate. There is an inherent discipline imposed by the authorized lectionary.

We have probably all heard the old joke about the lectionary. It starts with a giant meteor heading toward the earth which will destroy all life on the planet. There is nothing like the end of the world to get people out to church! So, all the churches are expecting big congregations that coming Sunday. As is their wont in jokes of this nature, a Baptist pastor, a Roman Catholic priest, and an Episcopal priest are all sitting around thinking about what text they will preach on. The Baptist pastor goes first. "This is easy," he says, "it has to be John 3:16—'For God so loved the world that he gave his only begotten son that whosoever believeth in him shall not perish but have everlasting life.' I'm going to bring people to Jesus."

The Roman Catholic priest goes next. "My text will be Matthew 16—'for on this rock' our Lord says to Peter 'I will build my church.' I will remind people that there is one true church in Christendom and it is important that you are right with Mother Church."

They both look at the Episcopal priest and wonder what text she will choose. Without hesitating, the priest replies: "I will preach on the lectionary readings of the day."

The lectionary is part of our discipline and part of our identity: we are one of the traditions that values the Word of God which is found in the lectionary. On a typical Sunday, four readings are part of worship in the Episcopal Church. Always, if there is a celebration of the Holy Eucharist, there is a reading from one of the four Gospels. The gospel is proclaimed and preached as part of our understanding of Word and sacrament. You could say that the Episcopal Church is a Bible-based church.

For whom are these two volumes written?

Words That Listen: A Literary Companion to the Lectionary is written for a large audience. The preacher will find literary and artistic treasures which open up the Gospels for the three-year lectionary cycle of the Church seasons and "ordinary" (that long season from Pentecost to Christ the King) time. The preacher will find literary allusions or images to enrich the homily or sermon. These books will not replace a careful exegesis or examination of the text, but they will remind the preacher that the words of Jesus Christ in the Gospels are in conversation with culture in every age.

The most effective preaching in the Episcopal Church is "Bible-based" but blessed with cultural texture and an appreciation for the gift of the Word, the power of words, and the joy of a well-crafted text. Several years ago, a newly ordained graduate from Virginia Theological Seminary settled into his new parish. I received a call from the rector who lamented that the newly minted priest understood biblical exegesis but failed to connect the dots for those listening to him and most often preached a Bible study rather than a sermon. He asked what could they do to help him. I suggested that they send him to Florence, Italy, and instruct him to look at Michelangelo's David for a week: an intense exercise in making room for beauty in the young preacher's mind and with his limited cultural experience. *Words That Listen* is a "culture trip" which affirms that indeed the Eternal Word was made flesh, very flesh.

For the person who wants to "hear" the gospel before the Sunday service, these two volumes will be a helpful companion—almost an expanded canon of sacred texts. For the person who is not following a lectionary, *Words That Listen* is an invitation to experience the ways the first-century Gospels have influenced great minds and faithful people.

The preacher and the person who is seeking a devotional resource should find the Gospels and their companion selections inspiring but not exhaustive or conclusive. Most of us need the inspiration of holy silence as much as we need additional words when it comes to gospel truth. Let this book not replace silent meditation but somehow encourage it as a practice for faithful reflection and living. Again, Wendell Berry is helpful. In his poem "How to be a Poet (to remind myself)" Berry celebrates the creativity of silence:

> Accept what comes from silence.
> Make the best you can of it.
> Of the little words that come
> out of the silence, like prayers
> prayed back to the one who prays,
> make a poem that does not disturb
> the silence from which it came.

We pray that these volumes will give the gift of silence as the Word and the words invite us to have a closer walk with our Lord and the God of all. For preachers and for the faithful listeners, *Words That Listen* is a companion to point the way for a richer engagement with the Incarnate Word and the God who breathed us all into being.

Lectionary preaching with literary and artistic companions

Perhaps it would be kind to offer an additional word to the preacher who will be using these volumes. How does one use a story or a poem in a sermon? Does it help always to name the source—or does that distract from the "flow" of the homily or sermon? Here is a portion of an ordination sermon which utilizes a scene from Flannery O'Connor's only novel, *Wise Blood*. The source is named in a footnote, but not in the sermon itself.

> "Nothing outside you can give you any place," it is said in *Wise Blood*. "You needn't look at the sky because it's not going to open up and show no place behind it. You needn't to search for any hole in the ground to look through into somewhere else. You can't go neither forwards nor backwards into your daddy's time nor your children's if you have them. In yourself right now is all the place you've got. If there was any Fall, look there, if there was any Redemption, look there, and if you expect any Judgment, look there, because they all three will have to be in your time and your body and where in your time and your body can they be?"
>
> In yourself now, as you are ordained a priest, you will spend the rest of your life proclaiming the mystery in yourself and in the Church of Fall, Judgment, and Redemption. You must throw "everything off balance" and hold up the host to a world that longs to be not displaced, not disabled. Hold up the host of wholeness to a broken world, the world God loves so much, in Jesus and now in us, his Body in the world.

Without actually quoting a poem, the preacher can appeal to the poetic imagination. In the following excerpt, I am clearly referring to several poems by W. H. Auden.

> Poets like Auden help me make sense out of this world, the Kingdom of Anxiety. I need beauty when the world is dull, dark, and ugly. The poet's words are like the morning light after a dark cold night. I need Bethlehem after Newtown. I need the one who is the Way, the Truth, and the Life. Today we make our feeble "Way" to Bethlehem where "Truth" was told and "Life" made everlasting for the whole of the human household.
>
> W. H. Auden takes us through the Word made Flesh, through Bethlehem, past the Newtowns of planet earth to "a great city that has expected your return for years." Let us be clear: our destination is not Bethlehem, nor is it any city that is home to the human household. No, we seek the One who waits for us in the New Jerusalem— the place where God is home and where there will be no tears, no sorrow but Life Everlasting. There is in the new Jerusalem a "bright clear day" for us and those we love.

The preacher's imagination is under a lot of pressure to offer thoughtful sermons and sermons which "feed the flock" Sunday after Sunday, week after week. These two volumes have some, but clearly not all, of the literary and artistic sources which could enrich gospel preaching. A final cautionary word: it is probably best for the preacher to be quite selective in utilizing additional or companion texts. Too many texts can obscure the preacher's own prose. A random text can be like a weed in a well-planned garden.

Sources for the literary and artistic selections

These two volumes reflect the actual practice of preaching. Most of the selections have been utilized to increase the preacher's imagination and interpretation of the gospel. The selections have been "tried." The writings of Early Church fathers and mothers have been included. The Anglican Divines are well represented. European and American (north and south) writers and artists are quoted. Films, novels, short stories, poems, and plays are matched to gospel texts—implying what Wendell Berry concludes that the Incarnate Word is "still speaking." Works of art remind us of the place of beauty in interpreting the Word which becomes flesh of our flesh.

Naturally, the task of picking this text over that is hard. Some are included because of their universal recognition—a volume like this must include some Shakespeare and some Dante. Some texts have a particular resonance with the Episcopal Church—so Flannery O'Connor and Martin Luther King Jr. speak to our situation in powerful ways. But we also wanted even the most literary Episcopalian to be stretched—so Jorge Luis Borges fantasy story "The Library of Babel" might be new or the theological implications of Leonard Cohen's haunting "Suzanne" might not have been noticed before. We have striven to make sure that women and men are included. Ancient and modern. Young and old. There are classics and there are some selections which are not well known at all. We sought to create and introduce our readers to an exciting and rich world.

The diversity of the literary and artistic selections is an attempt to "listen" to the universal appeal of the Good News which is in each of the four Gospels. Just as a crèche or nativity scene embodies or expresses its original context, so a selection from El Salvador will capture a gospel truth differently than a rural Anglican priest in Wales.

Concluding thoughts

My co-editor, Ian S. Markham, and I hope that readers of these two volumes will discover what we found in weaving this rich tapestry of literary gems. We learned that research is never a solitary task. We needed each other to explore the world of ideas which are informed by a first-century carpenter's son. There are times when we need someone to finish the thought we are having or the sentence we are writing.

Dean Markham and I also needed a community of thinkers to expand our ideas and to complete our project. So, we traveled to New York and Philadelphia to listen to Frank Griswold, the 25th Presiding Bishop of the Episcopal Church. His daily companions are the early church fathers and mothers. He introduced us in new ways to these timeless conversation partners and helped us connect them to various gospel texts and truths. Frank was, for us, a bridge to the wealth of the early church's encounter with the Risen Lord.

Mark Oakley introduced us to some contemporary English poets and writers. We met with him in a handsomely appointed room at St. Paul's Cathedral in London. He was a gracious host, taking us on a tour of that great cathedral of state occasions and opening his mind and heart to our research efforts. His own poetry graces our effort.

Our third consulting editor is the Very Reverend Cynthia Briggs Kittredge, the Dean and President at the Seminary of the Southwest. A number of Cynthia's literary companions are included in *Words That Listen*. She made sure the words of women were well represented, and we are delighted that two of her poems are included. After we met with Cynthia at Rather House, an arts and crafts house on the campus of the Seminary of the Southwest, she invited us to her lovely home for drinks on her porch.

During our visits with Frank, Mark, and Cynthia, our consulting editors shared the poems, short stories, novels, films and art which are part of their very being and daily life. They introduced us to old friends, ports in the storm of life. Wendell Berry advises that we "accept what comes from silence." Our consulting editors convinced us that good preaching and faithful meditation emerge from community and conversations deep and rich.

Our assisting editor is Greg Millikin, Associate Rector at St. Paul's Episcopal Church in Alexandria, Virginia. Greg secured the countless permissions needed. But more importantly, he brought a vast knowledge of films to our endeavor from his Generation Y perspective. His preaching is enhanced by his ability to connect films and pop culture references seen to the gospel heard on Sundays.

Cameron Soulis was a great help as the project started. A junior at Virginia Theological Seminary, Jean-Pierre Seguin, from the Diocese of Michigan, studied Spanish language and literature, history, and creative writing at the University of Michigan. Jean-Pierre has provided some of the rich Hispanic literature which graces our selections. We are also glad for his translation contributions. Brit Bjurstrom-Frazier also provided some helpful literary expertise towards the end of the project and contributed to the permissions. Finally, Ryan Masteller provided expertise and care as he nursed the project to completion.

Finally, the commissioning editor at Church Publishing, Davis Perkins, was involved in the project right at the beginning and was so helpful.

Most of us spend hours each day dealing with ordinary, mundane matters. We go to work; attend meetings; check emails;

deal with family and friends. It is a gift from time to time to put aside the claims of being in this world and live for a brief time in the world of ideas, even in the world of silence. We may be at our best when we live fully into being in God's image, appreciating quietly the creative, generative ideas and images which feed the human soul and keep us in touch with God and the world God loved so much. This book is such an invitation, such a hope for those who yearn to "hear" the gospel anew in their search for the Christ-like, well-formed life.

James Barney Hawkins IV
Advent 2016

Volume 1

Advent to Ascension

ADVENT 1

Matthew 24:36-44

Jesus said to the disciples, "But about that day and hour no one knows, neither the angels of heaven, nor the Son, but only the Father. For as the days of Noah were, so will be the coming of the Son of Man. For as in those days before the flood they were eating and drinking, marrying and giving in marriage, until the day Noah entered the ark, and they knew nothing until the flood came and swept them all away, so too will be the coming of the Son of Man. Then two will be in the field; one will be taken and one will be left. Two women will be grinding meal together; one will be taken and one will be left. Keep awake therefore, for you do not know on what day your Lord is coming. But understand this: if the owner of the house had known in what part of the night the thief was coming, he would have stayed awake and would not have let his house be broken into. Therefore you also must be ready, for the Son of Man is coming at an unexpected hour."

Year B

Mark 13:24-37

Jesus said to his disciples, "In those days, after that suffering, 'the sun will be darkened, and the moon will not give its light, and the stars will be falling from heaven, and the powers in the heavens will be shaken.' Then they will see 'the Son of Man coming in clouds' with great power and glory. Then he will send out the angels, and gather his elect from the four winds, from the ends of the earth to the ends of heaven. From the fig tree learn its lesson: as soon as its branch becomes tender and puts forth its leaves, you know that summer is near. So also, when you see these things taking place, you know that he is near, at the very gates. Truly I tell you, this generation will not pass away until all these things have taken place. Heaven and earth will pass away, but my words will not pass away. But about that day or hour no one knows, neither the angels in heaven, nor the Son, but only the Father. Beware, keep alert; for you do not know when the time will come. It is like a man going on a journey, when he leaves home and puts his slaves in charge, each with his work, and commands the doorkeeper to be on the watch. Therefore, keep awake—for you do not know when the master of the house will come, in the evening, or at midnight, or at cockcrow, or at dawn, or else he may find you asleep when he comes suddenly. And what I say to you I say to all: Keep awake."

Year C

Luke 21:25-36

Jesus said, "There will be signs in the sun, the moon, and the stars, and on the earth distress among nations confused by the roaring of the sea and the waves. People will faint from fear and foreboding of what is coming upon the world, for the powers of the heavens will be shaken. Then they will see 'the Son of Man coming in a cloud' with power and great glory. Now when these things begin to take place, stand up and raise your heads, because your redemption is drawing near." Then he told them a parable: "Look at the fig tree and all the trees; as soon as they sprout leaves you can see for yourselves and know that summer is already near. So also, when you see these things taking place, you know that the kingdom of God is near. Truly I tell you, this generation will not pass away until all things have taken place. Heaven and earth will pass away, but my words will not pass away. Be on guard so that your hearts are not weighed down with dissipation and drunkenness and the worries of this life, and that day catch you unexpectedly, like a trap. For it will come upon all who live on the face of the whole earth. Be alert at all times, praying that you may have the strength to escape all these things that will take place, and to stand before the Son of Man."

The famous *Left Behind* series of Tim LaHaye and Jerry B. Jenkins draws heavily on Matthew 24 as the text that describes the "rapture." Most mainline Christians are less worried about the world ending in a rapture and more worried about increasing secularization and the disappearance of religion. The Canadian novelist and artist, Douglas Campbell Coupland (b. 1961) is best known for his book *Generation X: Tales for an Accelerated Culture*. This essay comes from his collection of short stories called *Life After God*. The last story is called "1,000 Years (Life After God)." It is a reflection on the God gap in human lives. Starting with a group of teenagers in a swimming pool, we are taken through the stories of each human life—Mark tested positive for HIV, Stacey was now a "divorced aerobics instructor"—and culminates with our narrator admitting the purposelessness of their lives needs God. This extract is the start of the story and the end of the story.

> As suburban children we floated at night in swimming pools the temperature of blood; pools the color of Earth as seen from outer space. We would skinny-dip, my friends and me—hip-chick Stacey with her long yellow hair and Malibu Barbie body; Mark, our silent strongman; Kristy, our omni-freckled redheaded joke machine; voice-of-reason Julie, with the "statistically average" body; honey-bronze ski bum, Dana, with his nonexistent tan line and suspiciously large amounts of cash, and Todd, the prude, always last to strip, even then peeling off his underwear underneath the water. We would float and be naked—pretending to be embryos, pretending to be fetuses—all of us silent save for

the hum of the pool filter. Our minds would be blank and our eyes closed as we floated in warm waters, the distinction between our bodies and our brains reduced to nothing— bathed in chlorine and lit by pure blue lights installed underneath diving boards. Sometimes we would join hands and form a ring like astronauts in space; sometimes when we felt more isolated in our fetal stupor we would bump into each other in the deep end, like twins with whom we didn't even know we shared a womb.

Afterward we toweled off and drove in cars on roads that carved the mountain on which we lived—through the trees, through the subdivisions, from pool to pool, from basement to basement, up Cypress Bowl, down to Park Royal and over the Lions Gate Bridge—the act of endless motion itself a substitute for any larger form of thought. The radio would be turned on, full of love songs and rock music; we believed the rock music but I don't think we believed in the love songs, either then, or now. Ours was a life lived in paradise and thus it rendered any discussion of transcendental ideas pointless. Politics, we supposed, existed elsewhere in a televised non-paradise; death was something similar to recycling. Life was charmed but without politics or religion. It was the life of children of the children of the pioneers—life after God—a life of earthly salvation on the edge of heaven. Perhaps this is the finest thing to which we may aspire, the life of peace, the blurring between dream life and real life—and yet I find myself speaking these words with a sense of doubt.

I think there was a trade-off somewhere along the line. I think the price we paid for our golden life was an inability to fully believe in love; instead we gained an irony that scorched everything it touched. And I wonder if this irony is the price we paid for the loss of God. But then I must remind myself we are living creatures—we have religious impulses—we must—and yet into what cracks do these impulses flow in a world without religion? It is something I think about every day. Sometimes I think it is the only thing I should be thinking about....

[The end of the short story].

I peel my clothes and step into the pool beside the burbling stream, onto polished rocks, and water so clear that it seems it might not even be really there. My skin is grey, from lack of sun, from lack of bathing. And yes, the water is so cold, this water that only yesterday was locked as ice up on the mountaintops. But the pain from the cold is a pain that does not matter to me. I strip my pants, my shirt, my tie, my underwear and they lie strewn on the gravel bar next to my blanket. And the water from the stream above me roars.

Oh, does it roar! Like a voice that knows only one message, one truth—never-ending, like the clapping of hands and the cheers of the citizens upon the coronation of the king, the crowds of the inauguration, cheering for hope and for that one voice that will speak to them. Now—here is my secret: I tell it to you with an openness of heart that I doubt I shall ever achieve again, so I pray that you are in a quiet room as you hear these words.

My secret is that I need God—that I am sick and can no longer make it alone. I need God to help me give, because I no longer seem to be capable of giving; to help me be kind, as I no longer seem capable of kindness; to help me love, as I seem beyond being able to love.

The Gospels of Mark and Matthew exhort us to "keep awake." The theme of being awake is a key theme of Buddhism. The Buddha probably lived sometime between the sixth to the fourth centuries BCE. Here in this exchange, the Buddha explains that he is simply a person who knows the way things really are: he sees the ephemeral nature of all things.

My friend, what are you? Are you a celestial being
      or a god?
No, said the Buddha
Well, then, are you some kind of magician or wizard?
Again the Buddha answered, No
Are you a man? No
Well, my friend, then what are you?
the Buddha replied, I am awake

We start the Church year with three gospel readings all anticipating the incoming action of God in history. Langston Hughes (1902-1967) was an African American poet who asked the challenging question: why is the African American dream of equality and justice constantly deferred? In this 1951 poem, we have the agony of continuing oppression powerfully captured.

What happens to a dream deferred?

Does it dry up
like a raisin in the sun?
Or fester like a sore—
And then run?
Does it stink like rotten meat?
Or crust and sugar over—
like a syrupy sweet?

Maybe it just sags
like a heavy load.

Or does it explode?

All three gospel lessons in the Revised Common Lectionary begin the season of Advent with some sort of examination of eschatology; it sets the stage for why the Incarnation is necessary.

The film *Defending Your Life* (1991), written by its star, Albert Brooks (b. 1947), deals with judgment at the end of our earthly lives in a comedic way. Humans are judged by court-like panels on their lives in a heavenly rest-stop called "Judgment City." Daniel Miller (Brooks) has had to repeat life on Earth several times due to a sub-par existence. And the comic stakes are made even higher when the prosecutors who decide his judgment threaten to return him to Earth once again.

ADVENT 2

Matthew 3:1-12

In those days John the Baptist appeared in the wilderness of Judea, proclaiming, "Repent, for the kingdom of heaven has come near." This is the one of whom the prophet Isaiah spoke when he said, "The voice of one crying out in the wilderness: 'Prepare the way of the Lord, make his paths straight.'" Now John wore clothing of camel's hair with a leather belt around his waist, and his food was locusts and wild honey. Then the people of Jerusalem and all Judea were going out to him, and all the region along the Jordan, and they were baptized by him in the river Jordan, confessing their sins. But when he saw many Pharisees and Sadducees coming for baptism, he said to them, "You brood of vipers! Who warned you to flee from the wrath to come? Bear fruit worthy of repentance. Do not presume to say to yourselves, 'We have Abraham as our ancestor'; for I tell you, God is able from these stones to raise up children to Abraham. Even now the ax is lying at the root of the trees; every tree therefore that does not bear good fruit is cut down and thrown into the fire. I baptize you with water for repentance, but one who is more powerful than I is coming after me; I am not worthy to carry his sandals. He will baptize you with the Holy Spirit and fire. His winnowing fork is in his hand, and he will clear his threshing floor and will gather his wheat into the granary; but the chaff he will burn with unquenchable fire."

Year B

Mark 1:1-8

The beginning of the good news of Jesus Christ, the Son of God. As it is written in the prophet Isaiah, "See, I am sending my messenger ahead of you, who will prepare your way; the voice of one crying out in the wilderness: 'Prepare the way of the Lord, make his paths straight.'" John the baptizer appeared in the wilderness, proclaiming a baptism of repentance for the forgiveness of sins. And people from the whole Judean countryside and all the people of Jerusalem were going out to him, and were baptized by him in the river Jordan, confessing their sins. Now John was clothed with camel's hair, with a leather belt around his waist, and he ate locusts and wild honey. He proclaimed, "The one who is more powerful than I is coming after me; I am not worthy to stoop down and untie the thong of his sandals. I have baptized you with water; but he will baptize you with the Holy Spirit."

Year C

Luke 3:1-6

In the fifteenth year of the reign of Emperor Tiberius, when Pontius Pilate was governor of Judea, and Herod was ruler of Galilee, and his brother Philip ruler of the region of Ituraea and Trachonitis, and Lysanias ruler of Abilene, during the high priesthood of Annas and Caiaphas, the word of God came to John son of Zechariah in the wilderness. He went into all the region around the Jordan, proclaiming a baptism of repentance for the forgiveness of sins, as it is written in the book of the words of the prophet Isaiah, "The voice of one crying out in the wilderness: 'Prepare the way of the Lord, make his paths straight. Every valley shall be filled, and every mountain and hill shall be made low, and the crooked shall be made straight, and the rough ways made smooth; and all flesh shall see the salvation of God.'"

The second week of Advent is essentially devoted to the work of John the Baptist. Matthew starts with the phrase "Prepare the way of the Lord." *Godspell,* particularly David Haskell's (1948-2000) song "Prepare Ye the Way of the Lord," has popularized this biblical theme from Isaiah and from the pulpit of John. John the Baptist was Jesus's "warm-up," the part that is not on the program, not the first act. People came from all over the Judean countryside to be baptized, to repent, to be forgiven. The "way" by which John summoned was a way to the heart, a path straight to the heart, the interior preparation for the coming Messiah was by water. The Messiah will prepare by the Holy Spirit. John is Jesus's Holy Spirit, the one who made the way right for those who would follow the Man from Galilee.

It is worth dwelling on the start of Mark and on what is not covered. In Mark, there is no birth narrative. The Incarnation starts with the teacher not with the baby. Origen (185-254 CE) is one of the most creative early church theologians. Many of his teachings were considered highly innovative. In this excerpt from *On First Principles II.VI.2*, Origen muses on how "the man who appeared in Judaea" emerged from the miracle of the wisdom of God entering a woman's womb and producing a crying child.

> Of all the marvelous and splendid things about the Son of God there is one that utterly transcends the limits of human wonder and is beyond the capacity of our weak mortal intelligence to think of or understand, namely, how this mighty power of the divine majesty, the very Word of the Father, and the very Wisdom of God, in which were created "all things visible and invisible," can be believed to have existed within the compass of that man who appeared in Judaea; yes, and how the wisdom of God can have entered into a woman's womb and been born as a child and uttered noises like those of crying children; and further, how it was that he was troubled, as we are told, in the hour of death, as he himself confesses when he says, "My soul is sorrowful even unto death"; and how at the last he was led to that death which is considered by men to be the most shameful of all—even though on the third day he rose again.

Luke, along with Matthew and Mark, agree that John the Baptist comes from the wilderness. Louise Bogan (1897-1970) is an acute observer of the human condition, with a particular focus on issues facing women. In this poem, "Women," the image of wilderness seems to imply adventure, daring to step out, and daring to be different. Perhaps because society is oppressive, Bogan issues this challenge to women to live on the wild side.

Women have no wilderness in them,
They are provident instead,
Content in the tight hot cell of their hearts
To eat dusty bread.

They do not see cattle cropping red winter grass,
They do not hear
Snow water going down under culverts
Shallow and clear.

They wait, when they should turn to journeys,
They stiffen, when they should bend.
They use against themselves that benevolence
To which no man is friend.

They cannot think of so many crops to a field
Or of clean wood cleft by an axe.
Their love is an eager meaninglessness
Too tense, or too lax.

They hear in every whisper that speaks to them
A shout and a cry.
As like as not, when they take life over their door-sills
They should let it go by.

John the Baptist is not simply an important figure for Christianity. The Quran, the holy book of Islam, also recognizes his significance. In this passage from Chapter 19, John's birth from an elderly mother is recognized.

2. A mention of the mercy of your Lord towards His servant Zechariah.

3. When he called on his Lord, a call in seclusion.

4. He said, "My Lord, my bones have become feeble, and my hair is aflame with gray, and never, Lord, have I been disappointed in my prayer to you.

5. "And I fear for my dependents after me, and my wife is barren. So grant me, from Yourself, an heir.

6. To inherit me, and inherit from the House of Jacob, and make him, my Lord, pleasing."

7. "O Zechariah, We give you good news of a son, whose name is John, a name We have never given before."

8. He said, "My Lord, how can I have a son, when my wife is barren, and I have become decrepit with old age?"

9. He said, "It will be so, your Lord says, 'it is easy for me, and I created you before, when you were nothing.'"

10. He said, "My Lord, give me a sign." He said, "Your sign is that you will not speak to the people for three nights straight."

11. And he came out to his people, from the sanctuary, and signaled to them to praise morning and evening.

ADVENT 3

Matthew 11:2-11

When John heard in prison what the Messiah was doing, he sent word by his disciples and said to him, "Are you the one who is to come, or are we to wait for another?" Jesus answered them, "Go and tell John what you hear and see: the blind receive their sight, the lame walk, the lepers are cleansed, the deaf hear, the dead are raised, and the poor have good news brought to them. And blessed is anyone who takes no offense at me." As they went away, Jesus began to speak to the crowds about John: "What did you go out into the wilderness to look at? A reed shaken by the wind? What then did you go out to see? Someone dressed in soft robes? Look, those who wear soft robes are in royal palaces. What then did you go out to see? A prophet? Yes, I tell you, and more than a prophet. This is the one about whom it is written, 'See, I am sending my messenger ahead of you, who will prepare your way before you.' "Truly I tell you, among those born of women no one has arisen greater than John the Baptist; yet the least in the kingdom of heaven is greater than he."

Year B

John 1:6-8, 19-28

There was a man sent from God, whose name was John. He came as a witness to testify to the light, so that all might believe through him. He himself was not the light, but he came to testify to the light. This is the testimony given by John when the Jews sent priests and Levites from Jerusalem to ask him, "Who are you?" He confessed and did not deny it, but confessed, "I am not the Messiah." And they asked him, "What then? Are you Elijah?" He said, "I am not." "Are you the prophet?" He answered, "No." Then they said to him, "Who are you? Let us have an answer for those who sent us. What do you say about yourself?" He said, "I am the voice of one crying out in the wilderness, 'Make straight the way of the Lord,'" as the prophet Isaiah said. Now they had been sent from the Pharisees. They asked him, "Why then are you baptizing if you are neither the Messiah, nor Elijah, nor the prophet?" John answered them, "I baptize with water. Among you stands one whom you do not know, the one who is coming after me; I am not worthy to untie the thong of his sandal." This took place in Bethany across the Jordan where John was baptizing.

Year C

Luke 3:7-18

John said to the crowds that came out to be baptized by him, "You brood of vipers! Who warned you to flee from the wrath to come? Bear fruits worthy of repentance. Do not begin to say to yourselves, 'We have Abraham as our ancestor'; for I tell you, God is able from these stones to raise up children to Abraham. Even now the ax is lying at the root of the trees; every tree therefore that does not bear good fruit is cut down and thrown into the fire." And the crowds asked him, "What then should we do?" In reply he said to them, "Whoever has two coats must share with anyone who has none; and whoever has food must do likewise." Even tax collectors came to be baptized, and they asked him, "Teacher, what should we do?" He said to them, "Collect no more than the amount prescribed for you." Soldiers also asked him, "And we, what should we do?" He said to them, "Do not extort money from anyone by threats or false accusation, and be satisfied with your wages." As the people were filled with expectation, and all were questioning in their hearts concerning John, whether he might be the Messiah, John answered all of them by saying, "I baptize you with water; but one who is more powerful than I is coming; I am not worthy to untie the thong of his sandals. He will baptize you with the Holy Spirit and fire. His winnowing fork is in his hand, to clear his threshing floor and to gather the wheat into his granary; but the chaff he will burn with unquenchable fire." So, with many other exhortations, he proclaimed the good news to the people.

In Matthew, we have Jesus explaining that John the Baptist is "more than a prophet." So in this third week of Advent, we find the John the Baptist narrative developed as the identity is clarified. Thomas Merton (1915-1968) was a Catholic mystic who wrote extensively on spirituality and social justice. This is the third section of his poem, "St. John the Baptist." In this extract, we find the Baptist described in exalted terms—as the twin of Christ, with an amazing life which "laid down for us the form and pattern of our love for Christ."

> St. John, strong Baptist,
> Angel before the face of the Messiah
> Desert-dweller, knowing the solitudes that lie
> Beyond anxiety and doubt,
> Eagle whose flight is higher than our atmosphere
> Of hesitation and surmise,
> You are the first Cistercian and the greatest Trappist:
> Never abandon us, your few but faithful children,
> For we remember your amazing life,
> Where you laid down for us the form and pattern of
> Our love for Christ,
> Being so close to Him you were His twin.
> Oh buy us, by your intercession, in your mighty heaven,
> Not your great name, St. John, or ministry,
> But oh, your solitude and death:
> And most of all, gain us your great command of graces,
> Making our poor hands also fountains full of life and wonder
> Spending, in endless rivers, to the universe,
> Christ, in secret, and His Father, and His sanctifying Spirit.

In John, the Trinity hovers in the background of much of the Gospel. Ayodeji Malcolm Guite (b. 1957) is a poet, priest, academic, and songwriter. He was born of English parents in Nigeria and currently works at Girton College, Cambridge. His poem, "St. John the Baptist," is a description of the baptism of Jesus, where "the heavens opened" and we see the Holy Trinity at the heart of all things.

> Beginning here we glimpse the Three-in-one;
> The river runs, the clouds are torn apart,
> The Father speaks, the Spirit and the Son
> Reveal to us the single loving heart
> That beats behind the being of all things
> And calls and keeps and kindles us to light.
> The dove descends, the spirit soars and sings
> 'You are belovèd, you are my delight!'
> In that quick light and life, as water spills
> And streams around the Man like quickening rain,
> The voice that made the universe reveals
> The God in Man who makes it new again.
> He calls us too, to step into that river
> To die and rise and live and love forever.

Luke's picture of John the Baptist is demanding: he is clearly standing in the tradition of the eighth-century prophets of the Old Testament. Pastor Martin Niemöller (1892-1984) became a prophetic voice in Nazi Germany. He paid a significant price for his witness, spending seven years in concentration camps. His point is simple: without a prophetic voice that speaks up for the most vulnerable, there will not be a prophetic voice who will speak up when you are attacked.

> First they came for the Socialists,
> and I did not speak out—
> Because I was not a Socialist.
>
> Then they came for the Trade Unionists,
> and I did not speak out—
> Because I was not a Trade Unionist.
>
> Then they came for the Jews,
> and I did not speak out—
> Because I was not a Jew.
>
> Then they came for me—and there was no one left to speak for me.

The music of the monastic community in Taizé, France, has grown into an essential genre in Western Christian music in the last thirty years. Of Jacques Berthier's (1923-1994) many compositions, the canon "Prepare the Way of the Lord" is one of the more familiar selections during the Advent season, precisely because the sung choral round invites the listener and participant to meditate on the impact of John the Baptist's signature exclamation in the Gospels.

> Prepare the way of the Lord,
> prepare the way of the Lord,
> and all people will see
> the salvation of the Lord.

ADVENT 4

Matthew 1:18-25

Now the birth of Jesus the Messiah took place in this way. When his mother Mary had been engaged to Joseph, but before they lived together, she was found to be with child from the Holy Spirit. Her husband Joseph, being a righteous man and unwilling to expose her to public disgrace, planned to dismiss her quietly. But just when he had resolved to do this, an angel of the Lord appeared to him in a dream and said, "Joseph, son of David, do not be afraid to take Mary as your wife, for the child conceived in her is from the Holy Spirit. She will bear a son, and you are to name him Jesus, for he will save his people from their sins." All this took place to fulfill what had been spoken by the Lord through the prophet: "Look, the virgin shall conceive and bear a son, and they shall name him Emmanuel," which means, "God is with us." When Joseph awoke from sleep, he did as the angel of the Lord commanded him; he took her as his wife, but had no marital relations with her until she had borne a son; and he named him Jesus.

Year B

Luke 1:26-38

In the sixth month the angel Gabriel was sent by God to a town in Galilee called Nazareth, to a virgin engaged to a man whose name was Joseph, of the house of David. The virgin's name was Mary. And he came to her and said, "Greetings, favored one! The Lord is with you." But she was much perplexed by his words and pondered what sort of greeting this might be. The angel said to her, "Do not be afraid, Mary, for you have found favor with God. And now, you will conceive in your womb and bear a son, and you will name him Jesus. He will be great, and will be called the Son of the Most High, and the Lord God will give to him the throne of his ancestor David. He will reign over the house of Jacob forever, and of his kingdom there will be no end." Mary said to the angel, "How can this be, since I am a virgin?" The angel said to her, "The Holy Spirit will come upon you, and the power of the Most High will overshadow you; therefore the child to be born will be holy; he will be called Son of God. And now, your relative Elizabeth in her old age has also conceived a son; and this is the sixth month for her who was said to be barren. For nothing will be impossible with God." Then Mary said, "Here am I, the servant of the Lord; let it be with me according to your word." Then the angel departed from her.

Luke 1:39-45

In those days Mary set out and went with haste to a Judean town in the hill country, where she entered the house of Zechariah and greeted Elizabeth. When Elizabeth heard Mary's greeting, the child leaped in her womb. And Elizabeth was filled with the Holy Spirit and exclaimed with a loud cry, "Blessed are you among women, and blessed is the fruit of your womb. And why has this happened to me, that the mother of my Lord comes to me? For as soon as I heard the sound of your greeting, the child in my womb leaped for joy. And blessed is she who believed that there would be a fulfillment of what was spoken to her by the Lord."

The Gospel of Matthew provides the longest and most sustained description of the Annunciation. Henry Moore (1898-1986) is the sculptor of this masterpiece found at St. Paul's Cathedral in London. Entitled *Mother and Child* (1984), it depicts the mother and child entwined in a single block of marble. The form of both mother and child is made possible from the way the marble is carved so each figure lets the other emerge. Although Moore was skeptical about Christianity, he captures the mutual interdependence of mother and child.

The mystery of the Incarnation is beautifully captured in this remarkable poem. How exactly did man combine with God to create the Incarnation of God? The poetry of Ursula Askham Fanthorpe (known as U.A., 1929-2009) tries to take us inside Jesus. Here, in "Getting It Across," Fanthorpe invites us to look at the world through the eyes of Jesus—with disciples trying to hide their yawns, Jesus tries to convey the complexity of the Kingdom.

> 'His disciples said unto him, Lo, now speakest thou
> plainly, and speakest no proverb. Now are we sure that
> thou knowest all things.'
> St. John 16:29-30

> This is the hard thing.
> Not being God, the Son of Man,
> —I was born for that part—
> But patiently incising on these yokel faces,
> Mystified, bored and mortal,
> The vital mnemonics they never remember.

> There is enough of Man in my God
> For me to construe their frowns. I feel
> The jaw-cracking yawns they try to hide
> When out I come with one of my old
> Chestnuts. Christ! Not that bloody
> Sower again, they are saying, or God!
> Not the Prodigal bleeding Son.
> Give us a new one, for Messiah's sake.

> They know my unknowable parables as well
> As each other's shaggy dog stories.
> I say! I say! I say! There was this Samaritan,

This Philistine and this Roman...or
What did the high priest say
To the belly dancer? All they need
Is the cue for laughs. My sheep and goats,
Virgins, pigs, figtrees, loaves and lepers
Confuse them. Fishing, whether for fish or men,
Has unfitted them for analogy.

Yet these are my mouths. Through them only
Can I speak with Augustine, Aquinas, Martin, Paul
Regius Professors of Divinity,
And you, and you.
How can I cram the sense of Heaven's kingdom
Into our pidgin-Aramaic quayside jargon?

I envy Moses, who could choose
The diuturnity of stone for waymarks
Between man and Me. He broke the tablets,
Of course. I too know the easy messages
Are the ones not worth transmitting;
But he could at least carve.
The prophets too, however luckless
Their lives and instructions, inscribed on wood,
Papyrus, walls, their jaundiced oracles.

I alone must write on flesh. Not even
The congenial face of my Baptist cousin,
My crooked affinity Judas, who understands,
Men who would give me accurately to the unborn
As if I were something simple, like bread.
But Pete, with his headband stuffed with fishhooks,
His gift for rushing in where angels wouldn't,

Tom, for whom metaphor is anathema,
And James and John, who want the room at the top—
These numskulls are my medium. I called them.

I am tattooing God on their makeshift lives.
My Keystone Cops of disciples, always,
Running absurdly away, or lying ineptly,
Cutting off ears and falling into the water,
These Sancho Panzas must tread my Quixote life,
Dying ridiculous and undignified,
Flayed and stoned and crucified upside down.
They are the dear, the human, the dense, for whom
My message is. That might, had I not touched them,
Have died decent respectable upright deaths in bed.

In Luke, the mystery of divine connectivity is captured in the lives of two women. The Spanish mystic, St. John of the Cross (1542-1591), talks of the divine in terms of a fountain—a flowing spring—discovered in the darkness of the night. In this excerpt from "The Fountain," he culminates in linking the Incarnation with the Trinity with the mystery of the Holy Eucharist.

> I know well the fountain that flows and runs,
>> although it is night.
>
> That eternal spring is hidden,
> but well I know where has its dwelling,
>> even though it is night.
>
> I know that nothing can be as beautiful,
> and that the heavens and the earth drink of it,
>> even though it is night.
>
> I even know that in it no bottom can be found,
> and that none can afford it,
>> even though it is night.
>
> Its clearness is never darkened,
> and I know that all light comes from it,
>> even though it is night.
>
> I know its currents are so mighty,
> that they flow through hell, the heavens, and the peoples,
>> even though it is night.
>
> The current that flows from this spring,
> Oh, I know it is so capable and omnipotent,
>> even though it is night.

The current that from these two proceeds,
I know that neither of them it precede,
 even though it is night.

This eternal spring is hidden
in this living bread to give us life,
 even though it is night.

Here it is calling to the creatures,
and from this water they are satiated, although
 in darkness,
 because it is night.

This living spring that I desire,
in this bread of life, I see,
 even though it is night.

Translation by Jean-Pierre Seguin, 2017

The hope found in Mary in the Advent 4 lectionary has much to do with the power of belief and trust in God. This theological exploration is at the heart of the post-apocalyptic novel *The Children of Men*, by P.D. James (1920-2014). Later adapted into an award-winning film, the story focuses on a man compelled to protect a young pregnant woman from harm—the catch is that humanity is near extinction because no one has been able to conceive in decades. This unborn child may prove to be the last best hope for civilization and humanity. Riddled with incarnational allegory, the novel forces the reader to experience the emotions of a human race that wonders about God's providence—and reflects on the possibilities of God's care in the Incarnation.

"I don't think He bargains."

"Oh yes He does. I may not be religious but I know my Bible. My mother saw to that. He bargains all right. But He's supposed to be just. If He wants belief He'd better provide some evidence.'

"That He exists?"

"That He cares."

CHRISTMAS

Year A, B, and C

Luke 2:1-14(15-20)

In those days a decree went out from Emperor Augustus that all the world should be registered. This was the first registration and was taken while Quirinius was governor of Syria. All went to their own towns to be registered. Joseph also went from the town of Nazareth in Galilee to Judea, to the city of David called Bethlehem, because he was descended from the house and family of David. He went to be registered with Mary, to whom he was engaged and who was expecting a child. While they were there, the time came for her to deliver her child. And she gave birth to her firstborn son and wrapped him in bands of cloth, and laid him in a manger, because there was no place for them in the inn. In that region there were shepherds living in the fields, keeping watch over their flock by night. Then an angel of the Lord stood before them, and the glory of the Lord shone around them, and they were terrified. But the angel said to them, "Do not be afraid; for see—I am bringing you good news of great joy for all the people: to you is born this day in the city of David a Savior, who is the Messiah, the Lord. This will be a sign for you: you will find a child wrapped in bands of cloth and lying in a manger." And suddenly there was with the angel a multitude of the heavenly host, praising God and saying, "Glory to God in the highest heaven, and on earth peace among those whom he favors!" [When the angels had left them and gone into heaven, the shepherds said to one another, "Let us go now to Bethlehem and see this thing that has taken place, which the Lord has made known to us." So they went with haste and found Mary and Joseph, and the child lying in the manger. When they saw this, they made known what had been told them about this child; and all who heard it were amazed at what the shepherds told them. But Mary treasured all these words and pondered them in her heart. The shepherds returned, glorifying and praising God for all they had heard and seen, as it had been told them.]

The Lucan infancy narrative dominates the Christmas season because of the delicacy the evangelist takes in unfolding the story of the miraculous birth of a savior. G.K. Chesterton (1874-1936) had extensive interests: his much-loved novels involved Father Brown solving mysteries, and he was admired as a thoughtful exponent of orthodoxy. In these excerpts from his poem, "The Nativity," Chesterton affectionately sketches out the miracle of the Incarnation.

> The thatch of the roof was as golden,
> Though dusty the straw was and old,
> The wind was a peal as of trumpets,
> Though blowing and barren and cold.
> The mother's hair was a glory,
> Though loosened and torn,
> For under the eaves in the gloaming—
> A child was born.

Oh! if man sought a sign in the deepest,
That God shaketh broadest His best;
That things fairest, are oldest and simplest,
In the first days created and blest.
Far flush all the tufts of the clover,
Thick mellows the corn,
A cloud shapes, a daisy is opened—
A child is born.

Though the darkness be noisy with systems,
Dark fancies that fret and disprove;
Still the plumes stir around us, above us,
The wings of the shadow of love.
Still the fountains of life are unbroken,
Their splendour unshorn;
The secret, the symbol, the promise—
A child is born.

The wildly popular film *Avatar* (2009), written and directed by James Cameron (b. 1954), invited moviegoers into the foreign world of Pandora, where human beings could temporarily assume the bodies of the native Na'vi race. More than merely being deposited into this other world, the lead character Jake Sully begins to appreciate life amongst the Na'vi, ultimately choosing to become incarnate himself as one of them at the film's conclusion.

Luke captures the enormity of the Christmas moment as the heavens open and angels sing. Robert Browning (1812-1889) wrote this two-part poem, "Christmas-Eve" and "Easter Day," just after he had married Elizabeth Barrett Browning. In this poem, Robert Browning moves from a non-conformist church, to St. Peter's in Rome, to a lecture room where a professor is expounding a critical reading of Christian myths, back to this conclusion in the non-conformist church. One senses in this poem that Browning feels that churches are highly imperfect mediums to convey the majesty of the divine disclosure in the Incarnation.

And so we crossed the world and stopped.
For where am I, in city or plain,
Since I am 'ware of the world again?
And what is this that rises propped
With pillars of prodigious girth?
Is it really on the earth,
This miraculous Dome of God?
Has the angel's measuring-rod
Which numbered cubits, gem from gem,
'Twixt the gates of the New Jerusalem,
Meted it out,—and what he meted,
Have the sons of men completed?
—Binding, ever as he bade,
Columns in the colonnade
With arms wide open to embrace
The entry of the human race
To the breast of... what is it, yon building,
Ablaze in front, all paint and gilding,
With marble for brick, and stones of price

For garniture of the edifice?
Now I see; it is no dream;
It stands there and it does not seem;
For ever, in pictures, thus it looks,
And thus I have read of it in books
Often in England, leagues away,
And wondered how these fountains play,
Growing up eternally
Each to a musical water-tree,
Whose blossoms drop, a glittering boon,
Before my eyes, in the light of the moon,
To the granite layers underneath.
Liar and dreamer in your teeth!
I, the sinner that speak to you,
Was in Rome this night, and stood, and knew
Both this and more. For see, for see,
The dark is rent, mine eye is free
To pierce the crust of the outer wall,
And I view inside, and all there, all,
As the swarming hollow of a hive,
The whole Basilica alive!
Men in the chancel, body and nave,
Men on the pillars' architrave,
Men on the statues, men on the tombs
With popes and kings in their porphyry wombs,
All famishing in expectation
Of the main-altar's consummation.
For see, for see, the rapturous moment
Approaches, and earth's best endowment
Blends with heaven's; the taper-fires

Pant up, the winding brazen spires
Heave loftier yet the baldachin;*
The incense-gaspings, long kept in,
Suspire in clouds; the organ blatant
Holds his breath and grovels latent,
As if God's hushing finger grazed him,
(Like Behemoth when he praised him)
At the silver bell's shrill tinkling,
Quick cold drops of terror sprinkling
On the sudden pavement strewed
With faces of the multitude.
Earth breaks up, time drops away,
In flows heaven, with its new day
Of endless life, when He who trod,
Very man and very God,
This earth in weakness, shame and pain,
Dying the death whose signs remain
Up yonder on the accursed tree,—
Shall come again, no more to be
Of captivity the thrall,
But the one God, All in all,
King of kings, Lord of lords,
As His servant John received the words,
"I died, and live for evermore!

---

* Canopy over the High Altar

At the heart of the Christmas narrative is the Mother Mary placing the Christ Child in the manger, wrapped with care. The image of the Christ Child being wrapped with a shawl is suggestive of a short story by Cynthia Ozick (b. 1928). "The Shawl," first published in *The New Yorker* (May 26, 1980), is a rendering of the power of a shawl to protect a child in a concentration camp. Her Russian Jewish parents came to the United States fleeing the Russian state-organized pogroms against the Jews. The shawl plays a variety of roles in this moving short story. It implies danger, yet infinite shelter.

Stella, cold, cold, the coldness of hell. How they walked on the roads together, Rosa with Magda curled up between sore breasts, Magda wound up in the shawl. Sometimes Stella carried Magda. But she was jealous of Magda. A thin girl of fourteen, too small, with thin breasts of her own, Stella wanted to be wrapped in a shawl, hidden away, asleep, rocked by the march, a baby, a round infant in arms. Magda took Rosa's nipple, and Rosa never stopped walking, a walking cradle. There was not enough milk; sometimes Magda sucked air; then she screamed. Stella was ravenous. Her knees were tumors on sticks, her elbows chicken bones.

Rosa did not feel hunger; she felt light, not like someone walking but like someone in a faint, in trance, arrested in a fit, someone who is already a floating angel, alert and seeing everything, but in the air, not there, not touching the road. As if teetering on the tips of her fingernails. She looked into Magda's face through a gap in the shawl: a squirrel in a nest, safe, no one could reach her inside the little house of the shawl's windings. The face, very round, a pocket mirror of a face: but it was not Rosa's bleak complexion, dark like cholera, it was another kind of face altogether, eyes blue as air, smooth feathers of hair nearly as yellow as the Star sewn in to Rosa's coat. You could think she was one of *their* babies...

Rosa knew Magda was going to die very soon; she should have been dead already, but she had been buried away deep inside the magic shawl, mistaken there for the shivering mound of Rosa's breasts; Rosa clung to the shawl as if it covered only herself. No one took it away from her. Magda was mute. She never cried. Rosa hid her in the barracks, under the shawl, but she knew that one day someone would inform; or one day someone, not even Stella, would steal Magda to eat her. When Magda began to walk Rosa knew that Magda was going to die very soon, something would happen. She was afraid to fall asleep; she slept with the weight of her thigh on Magda's body; she was afraid she would smother Magda under her thigh. The weight of Rosa was becoming less and less; Rosa and Stella were slowly turning into air.

Magda was quiet, but her eyes were horribly alive, like blue tigers. She watched. Sometimes she laughed—it seemed a laugh, but how could it be? Magda had never seen anyone laugh. Still, Magda laughed at her shawl when the wind blew its corners, the bad wind with pieces of black in it, that made Stella's and Rosa's eyes tear. Magda's eyes were always clear and tearless. She watched like a tiger. She guarded her shawl. No one could touch it; only Rosa could touch it. Stella was not allowed. The shawl was Magda's own baby, her pet, her little sister. She tangled herself up in it and sucked on one of the corners when she wanted to be very still.

Then Stella took the shawl away and made Magda die.

Afterward Stella said: "I was cold." And afterward she was always cold, always. The cold went into her heart: Rosa saw that Stella's heart was cold...

All at once Magda was swimming through the air. The whole of Magda travelled through loftiness. She looked like a butterfly touching a silver vine. And the moment Magda's feathered round head and her pencil legs and balloonish belly and zigzag arms splashed against the fence, the steel voices went mad in their growling, urging Rosa to run and run to the spot where Magda had fallen from her flight against the electrified fence; but of course Rosa did not obey them. She only stood, because if she ran they would shoot, and if she tried to pick up the sticks of Magda's body they would shoot, and if she let the wolf's screech ascending now through the ladder of her skeleton break out, they would shoot; so she took Magda's shawl and filled her own mouth with it, stuffed it in and stuffed it in, until she was swallowing up the wolf's screech and tasting the cinnamon and almond depth of Magda's saliva; and Rosa drank Magda's shawl until it dried.

FIRST SUNDAY
AFTER CHRISTMAS

Year A, B, and C

John 1:1-18

In the beginning was the Word, and the Word was with God, and the Word was God. He was in the beginning with God. All things came into being through him, and without him not one thing came into being. What has come into being in him was life, and the life was the light of all people. The light shines in the darkness, and the darkness did not overcome it. There was a man sent from God, whose name was John. He came as a witness to testify to the light, so that all might believe through him. He himself was not the light, but he came to testify to the light. The true light, which enlightens everyone, was coming into the world. He was in the world, and the world came into being through him; yet the world did not know him. He came to what was his own, and his own people did not accept him. But to all who received him, who believed in his name, he gave power to become children of God, who were born, not of blood or of the will of the flesh or of the will of man, but of God. And the Word became flesh and lived among us, and we have seen his glory, the glory as of a father's only son, full of grace and truth. (John testified to him and cried out, "This was he of whom I said, 'He who comes after me ranks ahead of me because he was before me.'") From his fullness we have all received, grace upon grace. The law indeed was given through Moses; grace and truth came through Jesus Christ. No one has ever seen God. It is God the only Son, who is close to the Father's heart, who has made him known.

John's Gospel is unique for its cosmological theology, compared to the synoptics. It takes the bold position that the Second Person of the Trinity was preeminent before created time, and that the Incarnation has allowed that "Word" of God to take the form of flesh and blood. Terrence Malick's masterpiece, *The Tree of Life* (2011), is an art-house exploration in images and music of macro-theological themes such as those present in John 1. It is told primarily through the lens of a post-WWII American family, the O'Briens; in the present day the grown son Jack reflects on his childhood in snippets and flashes, culminating in a heartbreaking tragedy that forces him to confront his unresolved grief. But the film also takes a cosmic step back and looks at the experience of the human family in the context of the creation of the cosmos.

John Betjeman (1906-1984) is the author of the poem "Christmas." In these excerpts from the poem, there is this affectionate portrait of the charm of the typical Christmas scene which then culminates with a challenge. The final stanzas with their profound question—And is it true?—remind us of the dramatic claim of the Incarnation with its indelible connection to the Holy Eucharist.

The bells of waiting Advent ring,
The Tortoise stove is lit again
And lamp-oil light across the night
Has caught the streaks of winter rain.
In many a stained-glass window sheen
From Crimson Lake to Hooker's Green.

And is it true? and is it true?
The most tremendous tale of all,
Seen in a stained-glass window's hue,
A Baby in an ox's stall?
The Maker of the stars and sea
Become a Child on earth for me?

And is it true? For if it is,
No loving fingers tying strings
Around those tissued fripperies,
The sweet and silly Christmas things,
Bath salts and inexpensive scent
And hideous tie so kindly meant.

No love that in a family dwells,
No carolling in frosty air,
Nor all the steeple-shaking bells
Can with this single Truth compare—
That God was Man in Palestine
And lives to-day in Bread and Wine.

Brian Wren (b. 1936) is best known as a hymn-poet. He is a minister in the United Reformed Church. In this poem, "Good Is the Flesh," Wren captures the physicality of the Incarnation and reminds the reader that the Incarnation is the ultimate affirmation of the flesh and body.

Good is the flesh that the Word has become,
good is the birthing, the milk in the breast,
good is the feeding, caressing and rest,
good is the body for knowing the world,
Good is the flesh that the Word has become.
Good is the body for knowing the world,
sensing the sunlight, the tug of the ground,
feeling, perceiving, within and around,
good is the body, from cradle to grave,
Good is the flesh that the Word has become.
Good is the body, from cradle to grave,
growing and aging, arousing, impaired,
happy in clothing, or lovingly bared,
good is the pleasure of God in our flesh,
Good is the flesh that the Word has become.
Good is the pleasure of God in our flesh,
longing in all, as in Jesus, to dwell,
glad of embracing, and tasting, and smell,
good is the body, for good and for God,
Good is the flesh that the Word has become.

As we listen to the magisterial opening of John's Gospel, we should hear an echo of the opening of Genesis. "In the beginning . . . " is found at the start of both narratives. James Weldon Johnson (1871-1938) was the executive secretary of the National Association for the Advancement of Colored People from 1920 to 1930. He achieved several "firsts" for an American of African descent, including his appointment as professor at New York University. In this imaginative poetic exploration of creation, "The Creation," we are invited to see that God creates for the sake of company, and one way to look at John 1 is to see God's relationship with humanity being formed.

> And God stepped out on space,
> And he looked around and said:
> I'm lonely—
> I'll make me a world.
>
> And far as the eye of God could see
> Darkness covered everything,
> Blacker than a hundred midnights
> Down in a cypress swamp.
>
> Then God smiled,
> And the light broke,
> And the darkness rolled up on one side,
> And the light stood shining on the other,
> And God said: That's good!
>
> Then God reached out and took the light in his hands,
> And God rolled the light around in his hands
> Until he made the sun;
> And he set that sun a-blazing in the heavens.
> And the light that was left from making the sun

God gathered it up in a shining ball
And flung it against the darkness,
Spangling the night with the moon and stars.
Then down between
The darkness and the light
He hurled the world;
And God said: That's good!

SECOND SUNDAY AFTER CHRISTMAS

Year A, B, and C: Option 1

Matthew 2:13-15, 19-23

After the wise men had left, an angel of the Lord appeared to Joseph in a dream and said, "Get up, take the child and his mother, and flee to Egypt, and remain there until I tell you; for Herod is about to search for the child, to destroy him." Then Joseph got up, took the child and his mother by night, and went to Egypt, and remained there until the death of Herod. This was to fulfill what had been spoken by the Lord through the prophet, "Out of Egypt I have called my son." When Herod died, an angel of the Lord suddenly appeared in a dream to Joseph in Egypt and said, "Get up, take the child and his mother, and go to the land of Israel, for those who were seeking the child's life are dead." Then Joseph got up, took the child and his mother, and went to the land of Israel. But when he heard that Archelaus was ruling over Judea in place of his father Herod, he was afraid to go there. And after being warned in a dream, he went away to the district of Galilee. There he made his home in a town called Nazareth, so that what had been spoken through the prophets might be fulfilled, "He will be called a Nazorean."

Year A, B, and C: Option 2

Luke 2:41-52

The parents of Jesus went to Jerusalem every year for the festival of the Passover. And when he was twelve years old, they went up as usual for the festival. When the festival was ended and they started to return, the boy Jesus stayed behind in Jerusalem, but his parents did not know it. Assuming that he was in the group of travelers, they went a day's journey. Then they started to look for him among their relatives and friends. When they did not find him, they returned to Jerusalem to search for him. After three days they found him in the temple, sitting among the teachers, listening to them and asking them questions. And all who heard him were amazed at his understanding and his answers. When his parents saw him they were astonished; and his mother said to him, "Child, why have you treated us like this? Look, your father and I have been searching for you in great anxiety." He said to them, "Why were you searching for me? Did you not know that I must be in my Father's house?" But they did not understand what he said to them. Then he went down with them and came to Nazareth, and was obedient to them. His mother treasured all these things in her heart. And Jesus increased in wisdom and in years, and in divine and human favor.

Year A, B, and C: Option 3

Matthew 2:1-12

In the time of King Herod, after Jesus was born in Bethlehem of Judea, wise men from the East came to Jerusalem, asking, "Where is the child who has been born king of the Jews? For we observed his star at its rising, and have come to pay him homage." When King Herod heard this, he was frightened, and all Jerusalem with him; and calling together all the chief priests and scribes of the people, he inquired of them where the Messiah was to be born. They told him, "In Bethlehem of Judea; for so it has been written by the prophet: 'And you, Bethlehem, in the land of Judah, are by no means least among the rulers of Judah; for from you shall come a ruler who is to shepherd my people Israel.'" Then Herod secretly called for the wise men and learned from them the exact time when the star had appeared. Then he sent them to Bethlehem, saying, "Go and search diligently for the child; and when you have found him, bring me word so that I may also go and pay him homage." When they had heard the king, they set out; and there, ahead of them, went the star that they had seen at its rising, until it stopped over the place where the child was. When they saw that the star had stopped, they were overwhelmed with joy. On entering the house, they saw the child with Mary his mother; and they knelt down and paid him homage. Then, opening their treasure chests, they offered him gifts of gold, frankincense, and myrrh. And having been warned in a dream not to return to Herod, they left for their own country by another road.

The Holy Family's flight into Egypt has inspired many artists and writers. The Holy Family was fleeing Herod's wrath and the killing of the Holy Innocents. Joseph and Mary take Jesus, the Incarnation of innocence, and make the long journey to a foreign land, refugees on the run. Elliott Daingerfield's *Flight into Egypt* depicts a weary family at rest. Daingerfield, born in Harper's Ferry, West Virginia, in 1859, spent most of his prolific life painting in North Carolina.

In Luke's Gospel, the parents are anxious as their son, Jesus, goes about his heavenly Father's business. Saint Teresa of Avila (1515-1582) was a Spanish mystic and Carmelite nun. The prayer below became known as "St. Teresa's Bookmark" because it is believed that this was carried in her prayer book.

"Nada te turbe;	Let nothing disturb you;
nada te espante.	nothing frighten you.
Todo se pasa;	Everything is passing;
Dios no se muda.	God does not change.
La paciencia	Patience accomplishes
todo lo alcanza.	all things.
Quien a Dios tiene,	The one who has God
nada le falta.	lacks nothing.
Solo Dios basta."	God alone suffices.

Translation by Jean-Pierre Seguin, 2016

The two passages from Matthew capture the fear of Herod and his violent reaction. Yet the divine action in Christ is an invitation to live in peace with each other. Maya Angelou (1928-2014) was a civil rights activist, author, and poet. She is best known for her seven autobiographies, which describe her childhood and early adult life. Angelou stresses the hope of Christmas and the peaceful injunction in her poem "Amazing Peace."

> We clap hands and welcome the Peace of Christmas.
> We beckon this good season to wait a while with us.
> We, Baptist and Buddhist, Methodist and Muslim, say come.
> Peace.
>
> Come and fill us and our world with your majesty.
> We, the Jew and the Jainist, the Catholic and the Confucian,
> Implore you, to stay a while with us.
> So we may learn by your shimmering light
> How to look beyond complexion and see community.

The aspiration to flee to survive is deep in the human psyche. In the film *El Norte* (1983), we see a Mayan Indian peasant fleeing the Guatemalan Army to get to Mexico in the hope of getting to America. At every stage he has the challenge of assimilation. To begin with, he needs to first pass as a Mexican to be able to get to Mexico; in one comic exchange, he has to receive advice even on how to act "Mexican." But at its heart, *El Norte* is a companion to the flight to Egypt of Mary and Joseph: a compassionate story about the hardships and hope on the path towards crossing the border into "El Norte" (the USA) itself.

FEAST OF THE EPIPHANY

Year A, B, and C

Matthew 2:1-12

In the time of King Herod, after Jesus was born in Bethlehem of Judea, wise men from the East came to Jerusalem, asking, "Where is the child who has been born king of the Jews? For we observed his star at its rising, and have come to pay him homage." When King Herod heard this, he was frightened, and all Jerusalem with him; and calling together all the chief priests and scribes of the people, he inquired of them where the Messiah was to be born. They told him, "In Bethlehem of Judea; for so it has been written by the prophet: 'And you, Bethlehem, in the land of Judah, are by no means least among the rulers of Judah; for from you shall come a ruler who is to shepherd my people Israel.'" Then Herod secretly called for the wise men and learned from them the exact time when the star had appeared. Then he sent them to Bethlehem, saying, "Go and search diligently for the child; and when you have found him, bring me word so that I may also go and pay him homage." When they had heard the king, they set out; and there, ahead of them, went the star that they had seen at its rising, until it stopped over the place where the child was. When they saw that the star had stopped, they were overwhelmed with joy. On entering the house, they saw the child with Mary his mother; and they knelt down and paid him homage. Then, opening their treasure chests, they offered him gifts of gold, frankincense, and myrrh. And having been warned in a dream not to return to Herod, they left for their own country by another road.

Maya Angelou (1928-2014) was a civil rights activist, author, and poet. In this poem, "Alone," she invites the reader to some serious self-examination. Instead of pursuing money, we need to connect with family and friends. In so doing, she taps into that central Epiphany theme that God is coming for all of us, for "Nobody, but nobody can make it out here alone."

Lying, thinking
Last night
How to find my soul a home
Where water is not thirsty
And bread loaf is not stone
I came up with one thing
And I don't believe I'm wrong
That nobody,
But nobody
Can make it out here alone.

Alone, all alone
Nobody, but nobody
Can make it out here alone.

There are some millionaires
With money they can't use
Their wives run round like banshees
Their children sing the blues

They've got expensive doctors
To cure their hearts of stone.
But nobody
No, nobody
Can make it out here alone.

Alone, all alone
Nobody, but nobody
Can make it out here alone.

Now if you listen closely
I'll tell you what I know
Storm clouds are gathering
The wind is gonna blow
The race of man is suffering
And I can hear the moan,
'Cause nobody,
But nobody
Can make it out here alone.

Alone, all alone
Nobody, but nobody
Can make it out here alone.

Lewis Carroll's (1832-1898) famous story *Alice's Adventures in Wonderland* has captured the imagination of children for generations. With the gospel focused on the journey of the wise men from the East, we find Lewis Carroll playing around with the paradox of a journey and a destination in this lovely exchange between Alice and the Cheshire Cat. Do note how the math don at Oxford, playfully, brings his skills as a logician into play.

"Cheshire Puss," she began, rather timidly, as she did not at all know whether it would like the name: however, it only grinned a little wider. "Come, it's pleased so far," thought Alice, and she went on. "Would you tell me, please, which way I ought to go from here?"

"That depends a good deal on where you want to get to," said the Cat.

"I don't much care where —" said Alice.

"Then it doesn't matter which way you go," said the Cat.

" — so long as I get somewhere," Alice added as an explanation.

"Oh, you're sure to do that," said the Cat, "if you only walk long enough."

Alice felt that this could not be denied, so she tried another question. "What sort of people live about here?"

"In that direction," the Cat said, waving its right paw around, "lives a Hatter: and in that direction," waving the other paw, "lives a March Hare. Visit either you like: they're both mad."

"But I don't want to go among mad people," Alice remarked.

"Oh, you can't help that," said the Cat: "we're all mad here. I'm mad. You're mad."

"How do you know I'm mad?" said Alice.

"You must be," said the Cat, "or you wouldn't have come here."

Alice didn't think that proved it at all; however, she went on, "And how do you know that you're mad?"

"To begin with," said the Cat, "a dog's not mad. You grant that?"

"I suppose so," said Alice.

"Well then," the Cat went on, "you see, a dog growls when it's angry, and wags its tail when it's pleased. Now I growl when I'm pleased, and wag my tail when I'm angry. Therefore I'm mad."

"I call it purring, not growling," said Alice.

"Call it what you like," said the Cat.

The kings arrive bearing their famous gifts. William Carlos Williams (1883-1963) was a doctor who was also a poet. As a poet, he was part of a group linked with modernism and imagism. This poem, "The Gift," captures the paradox of such extravagant gifts when the miracle is the perfect child drinking from his mother's breast.

As the wise men of old brought gifts
    guided by a star
        to the humble birthplace
of the god of love,
    the devils
        as an old print shows
retreated in confusion.
    What could a baby know
        of gold ornaments
or frankincense and myrrh,
    of priestly robes
        and devout genuflections?
But the imagination
    knows all stories
        before they are told
and knows the truth of this one
    past all defection
The rich gifts
    so unsuitable for a child
        though devoutly proffered,
stood for all that love can bring.
    The men were old
        how could they know

of a mother's needs
  or a child's
    appetite?
But as they kneeled
  the child was fed.
    They saw it
and
  gave praise!
    A miracle
had taken place,
  hard gold to love,
a mother's milk!
  before
    their wondering eyes.
The ass brayed
  the cattle lowed.
    It was their nature.
All men by their nature give praise.
  It is all
    they can do.
The very devils
  by their flight give praise.
    What is death,
beside this?
  Nothing. The wise men
    came with gifts
and bowed down
  to worship
    this perfection.

The wise men from the East are on a search. There is a deep sense of competing desires in this gospel—for Herod, a desire of fear; for the wise men, a desire of hope. Federico García Lorca (1898-1936) is best known as a Spanish poet who was part of the famous Generation of '27. This was a group that incorporated into Spanish literature certain features of the European literary avant-garde, such as symbolism and futurism. Here, however, in "The Casida of the Rose," Lorca uses the classical Arabic *qasida* form to capture the mystery of desire—the aching quest and journey.

> The rose
> was not searching for the sunrise:
> almost eternal on its branch,
> it was searching for something else.
>
> The rose
> was not searching for darkness or science:
> borderline of flesh and dream,
> it was searching for something else.
>
> The rose
> was not searching for the rose.
> Motionless in the sky
> it was searching for something else.

Translated by Robert Bly

THE FIRST SUNDAY AFTER THE EPIPHANY: THE FEAST OF THE BAPTISM OF OUR LORD

Year A

Matthew 3:13-17

Jesus came from Galilee to John at the Jordan, to be baptized by him. John would have prevented him, saying, "I need to be baptized by you, and do you come to me?" But Jesus answered him, "Let it be so now; for it is proper for us in this way to fulfill all righteousness." Then he consented. And when Jesus had been baptized, just as he came up from the water, suddenly the heavens were opened to him and he saw the Spirit of God descending like a dove and alighting on him. And a voice from heaven said, "This is my Son, the Beloved, with whom I am well pleased."

Year B

Mark 1:4-11

John the baptizer appeared in the wilderness, proclaiming a baptism of repentance for the forgiveness of sins. And people from the whole Judean countryside and all the people of Jerusalem were going out to him, and were baptized by him in the river Jordan, confessing their sins. Now John was clothed with camel's hair, with a leather belt around his waist, and he ate locusts and wild honey. He proclaimed, "The one who is more powerful than I is coming after me; I am not worthy to stoop down and untie the thong of his sandals. I have baptized you with water; but he will baptize you with the Holy Spirit." In those days Jesus came from Nazareth of Galilee and was baptized by John in the Jordan. And just as he was coming up out of the water, he saw the heavens torn apart and the Spirit descending like a dove on him. And a voice came from heaven, "You are my Son, the Beloved; with you I am well pleased."

Year C

Luke 3:15-17, 21-22

As the people were filled with expectation, and all were questioning in their hearts concerning John, whether he might be the Messiah, John answered all of them by saying, "I baptize you with water; but one who is more powerful than I is coming; I am not worthy to untie the thong of his sandals. He will baptize you with the Holy Spirit and fire. His winnowing fork is in his hand, to clear his threshing floor and to gather the wheat into his granary; but the chaff he will burn with unquenchable fire." Now when all the people were baptized, and when Jesus also had been baptized and was praying, the heaven was opened, and the Holy Spirit descended upon him in bodily form like a dove. And a voice came from heaven, "You are my Son, the Beloved; with you I am well pleased."

Baptism pervades all three of the lectionary readings. Anne Lamott (b. 1954) is an American writer and political activist. In her book *Grace (Eventually): Thoughts on Faith*, Lamott provides a beautiful description of baptism—an act of letting go and getting drenched.

> Christianity is *about* water: "Everyone that thirsteth, come ye to the waters." It's about baptism, for God's sake. It's about full immersion, about falling into something elemental and *wet*. Most of what we do in worldly life is geared toward our staying dry, looking good, not going under. But in baptism, in lakes and rain and tanks and fonts, you agree to do something that's a little sloppy because at the same time it's also holy, and absurd. It's about surrender, giving in to all those things we can't control; it's a willingness to let go of balance and decorum and get *drenched*.

The Gospel of Mark explains that John was "proclaiming a baptism of repentance." Anthony Burgess wrote *A Clockwork Orange* in 1962. The story of Alex, a 15-year old schoolboy who leads a gang of Peter, Georgie, and Dim, engages in gratuitous violence in a drug-oriented world. The book ends up being a study in the complex relationship between violence, treatment, and human identity. It was made into a film, which followed the American edition, where the last chapter of Burgess' book was dropped. Instead of Alex being resolved to settle down and find a girl; we are left with the angry Alex ready to reassert himself through violence. In the English edition, we have a repentant Alex (in the sense that he is tired of a life of perpetual violence); in the American edition, we have an Alex who in the end cannot change. This is an extract from the repentant Alex, where he meets Peter and wants the normalcy of a marriage (do note how Burgess creates an entire language for his futuristic gang world—so translations are provided by the editors).

"This," said Pete to the devotchka [girl], "is an old friend. His name is Alex. May I," he said to me, "introduce my wife?"

My rot fell wide open then. "Wife?" I like gaped. "Wife, wife wife? Ah no, that cannot be. Too young art thou to be married, old droog [friend]. Impossible impossible." ...

Perhaps that was it, I kept thinking. Perhaps I was getting too old for the sort of jeezny [life] I had been leading, brothers. ... Walking the dark chill bastards of winter streets after ittying off from this chai and coffee mesto, I kept viddying like visions, like these cartoons in the gazettas. … But I had this sudden very strong idea that if I walked into the room next to this room where the fire was burning away and my hot dinner laid on the table, there I should find what I really wanted, and now it all tied up, that picture scissored out of the gazetta and meeting old Pete like that. For in that other room in a cot was laying gurgling goo goo goo my son. …

A terribly grazhny [dirty] vonny [smelly] world, really, O my brothers. And so farewell to you from your little droog. And to all others in this story profound shooms [noises] of lip music brrrrr. And they can kiss my sharries. But you, O my brothers, remember sometimes thy little Alex that was. Amen. And all that cal.

Luke's baptism narrative is very visual, with plenty of dialogue. Joel and Ethan Coen's film *O Brother, Where Art Thou?* (2000) follows three hapless escaped convicts in 1930s Mississippi, on the hunt for a lost treasure. In one key memorable sequence in the film, Emmett, Pete, and Delmar stumble upon a religious sect in the woods participating in a full-immersion baptismal rite with its newest members. Delmar even gets swept up into the action and is baptized along with the throngs, in an elegiac series of images set to Alison Krauss' haunting "Down to the River to Pray."

Mark's Gospel begins with the preaching of John the Baptist. Then John baptizes Jesus and immediately Jesus is tempted. There follows Jesus's ministry in Galilee. Ministry follows baptism. Flannery O'Connor (1925-1964) includes the scandalous baptism of Harry Ashfield in her short story, "The River." Young Harry did not "count" before. His life was an "ash field" without being washed in the River Jordan.

"If I Baptize you," the preacher said, "you'll be able to go to the Kingdom of Christ. You'll be washed in the river of suffering, son, and you'll go by the deep river of life. Do you want that?"

"Yes," the child said, and thought, I won't go to the apartment then, I'll go under the river.

"You won't be the same again," the preacher said. "You'll count." . . .

Suddenly the preacher said, "All right, I'm going to Baptize you now," and without more warning, he tightened his hold and swung him upside down and plunged his head into the water. He held him under while he said the words of Baptism and then he jerked him up again and looked sternly at the gasping child. [The child's] eyes were dark and dilated. "You count now," the preacher said. "You didn't even count before."

THE SECOND SUNDAY
AFTER THE EPIPHANY

Year A

John 1:29-42

John saw Jesus coming toward him and declared, "Here is the Lamb of God who takes away the sin of the world! This is he of whom I said, 'After me comes a man who ranks ahead of me because he was before me.' I myself did not know him; but I came baptizing with water for this reason, that he might be revealed to Israel." And John testified, "I saw the Spirit descending from heaven like a dove, and it remained on him. I myself did not know him, but the one who sent me to baptize with water said to me, 'He on whom you see the Spirit descend and remain is the one who baptizes with the Holy Spirit.' And I myself have seen and have testified that this is the Son of God." The next day John again was standing with two of his disciples, and as he watched Jesus walk by, he exclaimed, "Look, here is the Lamb of God!" The two disciples heard him say this, and they followed Jesus. When Jesus turned and saw them following, he said to them, "What are you looking for?" They said to him, "Rabbi" (which translated means Teacher), "where are you staying?" He said to them, "Come and see." They came and saw where he was staying, and they remained with him that day. It was about four o'clock in the afternoon. One of the two who heard John speak and followed him was Andrew, Simon Peter's brother. He first found his brother Simon and said to him, "We have found the Messiah" (which is translated Anointed). He brought Simon to Jesus, who looked at him and said, "You are Simon son of John. You are to be called Cephas" (which is translated Peter).

Year B

John 1:43-51

Jesus decided to go to Galilee. He found Philip and said to him, "Follow me." Now Philip was from Bethsaida, the city of Andrew and Peter. Philip found Nathanael and said to him, "We have found him about whom Moses in the law and also the prophets wrote, Jesus son of Joseph from Nazareth." Nathanael said to him, "Can anything good come out of Nazareth?" Philip said to him, "Come and see." When Jesus saw Nathanael coming toward him, he said of him, "Here is truly an Israelite in whom there is no deceit!" Nathanael asked him, "Where did you get to know me?" Jesus answered, "I saw you under the fig tree before Philip called you." Nathanael replied, "Rabbi, you are the Son of God! You are the King of Israel!" Jesus answered, "Do you believe because I told you that I saw you under the fig tree? You will see greater things than these." And he said to him, "Very truly, I tell you, you will see heaven opened and the angels of God ascending and descending upon the Son of Man."

Year C

John 2:1-11

On the third day there was a wedding in Cana of Galilee, and the mother of Jesus was there. Jesus and his disciples had also been invited to the wedding. When the wine gave out, the mother of Jesus said to him, "They have no wine." And Jesus said to her, "Woman, what concern is that to you and to me? My hour has not yet come." His mother said to the servants, "Do whatever he tells you." Now standing there were six stone water jars for the Jewish rites of purification, each holding twenty or thirty gallons. Jesus said to them, "Fill the jars with water." And they filled them up to the brim. He said to them, "Now draw some out, and take it to the chief steward." So they took it. When the steward tasted the water that had become wine, and did not know where it came from (though the servants who had drawn the water knew), the steward called the bridegroom and said to him, "Everyone serves the good wine first, and then the inferior wine after the guests have become drunk. But you have kept the good wine until now." Jesus did this, the first of his signs, in Cana of Galilee, and revealed his glory; and his disciples believed in him.

The Jesus of John's Gospel is cosmic. The God of the call, the God of the baptism, is remarkable. R.S. Thomas (1913-2000) invites us, in this poem, "Raptor," to believe in the enormous God of John's Gospel.

You have made God small,
Setting him aside
A pipette or a retort
Studying the bubbles,
Absorbed in an experiment
That will come to nothing.

I think of him rather
As an enormous owl
Abroad in the shadows,
Brushing me sometimes
With his wing so the blood
In my veins freezes, able

To find his way from one
Soul to another because
He can see in the dark.
I have heard him crooning
To himself, so that almost
I could believe in angels,

Those feathered overtones
In love's rafters, I have heard
Him scream too, fastening
His talons in his great
Adversary, or in some lesser
Denizen, maybe, like you or me.

Francis Thompson (1859-1907) was an English poet who was saved by his poetry. He is best known for his poem "The Hound of Heaven." This poem, "In No Strange Land (The Kingdom of God is Within You)" was written in the 1880s, when he was homeless and addicted to opium. He would sleep outside at Charing Cross junction. In the same way that fish do not question the existence of the sea, so we should not question the existence of God. As John 1:51, there is an allusion to Jacob's ladder (Genesis 28), here the poet explains that heaven is constantly meeting earth all around us.

O world invisible, we view thee,
O world intangible, we touch thee,
O world unknowable, we know thee,
Inapprehensible, we clutch thee!

Does the fish soar to find the ocean,
The eagle plunge to find the air—
That we ask of the stars in motion
If they have rumor of thee there?

Not where the wheeling systems darken,
And our benumbed conceiving soars!—
The drift of pinions, would we hearken,
Beats at our own clay-shuttered doors.

The angels keep their ancient places—
Turn but a stone and start a wing!
'Tis ye, 'tis your estrangèd faces,
That miss the many-splendored thing.

But (when so sad thou canst not sadder)
Cry—and upon thy so sore loss
Shall shine the traffic of Jacob's ladder
Pitched betwixt Heaven and Charing Cross.

Yea, in the night, my Soul, my daughter,
Cry—clinging to Heaven by the hems;
And lo, Christ walking on the water,
Not of Gennesareth, but Thames!

The first miracle in John's Gospel is the wedding at Cana. Malcolm Guite (b. 1957) is a poet, priest, academic, and songwriter, who captures the beauty of this moment in his poem, "Epiphany at Cana." In the simplicity of the miracle, which can be enjoyed with ease on the tongue, Guite reminds us that it cost our Savior everything.

Here's an epiphany to have and hold,
A truth that you can taste upon the tongue,
No distant shrines and canopies of gold
Or ladders to be clambered rung by rung,
But here and now, amidst your daily living,
Where you can taste and touch and feel and see,
The spring of love, the fount of all forgiving,
Flows when you need it, rich, abundant, free.

Better than waters of some outer weeping,
That leave you still with all your hidden sin,
Here is a vintage richer for the keeping
That works its transformation from within.
"What price?" you ask me, as we raise the glass,
"It cost our Saviour everything he has."

In Stephen King's (b. 1947) remarkable classic *The Stand*, a human-made plague wipes out 99.4 percent of the planet; the survivors, who find themselves immune to this virus, then divide into two disparate sects—one good and one evil. The call to a particular force of good or evil comes in the form of dreams and visions of two diametrically opposed figures—the saintly, elderly, African American Mother Abigail in Nebraska or the frightening Randall Flagg. When the deaf-mute character Nick and friend Ralph meet Abigail in this sequence, Nick expresses his concern about this mission they are called to follow.

> She shook her head patiently. "Nick, all things serve the Lord. Don't you think this black man serves Him, too? He does, no matter how mysterious His purpose may be. The black man will follow you no matter where you run, because he serves the purpose of God, and God wants you to treat with him. It don't do no good to run from the will of the Lord God of Hosts. A man or woman who tries that only ends up in the belly of the beast."

Nick wrote briefly. Ralph studied the note, rubbed the side of his nose, and wished he didn't have to read it. Old ladies like this didn't cotton to stuff like what Nick had just written. She'd likely call it a blasphemy, and shout it loud enough to wake everyone in the place, too.

"What's he say?" Abigail asked.

"He says . . ." Ralph cleared his throat; the feather stuck in the band of his hat jiggled. "He says that he don't believe in God." The message relayed, he looked unhappily down at his shoes and waited for the explosion.

But she only chuckled, got up, and walked across to Nick. She took one of his hands and patted it. "Bless you, Nick, but that don't matter. He believes in you."

THE THIRD SUNDAY AFTER THE EPIPHANY

Year A

Matthew 4:12-23

When Jesus heard that John had been arrested, he withdrew to Galilee. He left Nazareth and made his home in Capernaum by the sea, in the territory of Zebulun and Naphtali, so that what had been spoken through the prophet Isaiah might be fulfilled: "Land of Zebulun, land of Naphtali, on the road by the sea, across the Jordan, Galilee of the Gentiles—the people who sat in darkness have seen a great light, and for those who sat in the region and shadow of death light has dawned." From that time Jesus began to proclaim, "Repent, for the kingdom of heaven has come near." As he walked by the Sea of Galilee, he saw two brothers, Simon, who is called Peter, and Andrew his brother, casting a net into the sea—for they were fishermen. And he said to them, "Follow me, and I will make you fish for people." Immediately they left their nets and followed him. As he went from there, he saw two other brothers, James son of Zebedee and his brother John, in the boat with their father Zebedee, mending their nets, and he called them. Immediately they left the boat and their father, and followed him. Jesus went throughout Galilee, teaching in their synagogues and proclaiming the good news of the kingdom and curing every disease and every sickness among the people.

Year B

Mark 1:14-20

After John was arrested, Jesus came to Galilee, proclaiming the good news of God, and saying, "The time is fulfilled, and the kingdom of God has come near; repent, and believe in the good news." As Jesus passed along the Sea of Galilee, he saw Simon and his brother Andrew casting a net into the sea—for they were fishermen. And Jesus said to them, "Follow me and I will make you fish for people." And immediately they left their nets and followed him. As he went a little farther, he saw James son of Zebedee and his brother John, who were in their boat mending the nets. Immediately he called them; and they left their father Zebedee in the boat with the hired men, and followed him.

Year C

Luke 4:14-21

Jesus, filled with the power of the Spirit, returned to Galilee, and a report about him spread through all the surrounding country. He began to teach in their synagogues and was praised by everyone. When he came to Nazareth, where he had been brought up, he went to the synagogue on the Sabbath day, as was his custom. He stood up to read, and the scroll of the prophet Isaiah was given to him. He unrolled the scroll and found the place where it was written: "The Spirit of the Lord is upon me, because he has anointed me to bring good news to the poor. He has sent me to proclaim release to the captives and recovery of sight to the blind, to let the oppressed go free, to proclaim the year of the Lord's favor." And he rolled up the scroll, gave it back to the attendant, and sat down. The eyes of all in the synagogue were fixed on him. Then he began to say to them, "Today this scripture has been fulfilled in your hearing."

Matthew and Mark are both focused on the invitation to follow Jesus. Reynolds Price (1933-2011) was the James B. Duke Professor of English at Duke University and also a poet and novelist. The excerpt from *A Whole New Life: An Illness and a Healing* describes a mystical experience that he had on July 3, 1984, while being treated for a cancerous tumor. Price follows Jesus into the river, where his sins are forgiven.

I saw it was Jesus, bound toward me. He looked much like the lean Jesus of Flemish paintings—tall with dark hair, unblemished skin and a self-possession both natural and imposing.

Again I felt no shock or fear. All this was normal human event; it was utterly clear to my normal eyes and was happening as surely as any event of my previous life. I lay and watched him walk on nearer.

Jesus bent and silently beckoned me to follow.

I knew to shuck off my trousers and jacket, then my shirt and shorts. Bare, I followed him.

Jesus silently took up handfuls of water and poured them over my head and back till water ran down my puckered scar. Then he spoke once—"Your sins are forgiven"—and turned to shore again, done with me.

I came on behind him, thinking in standard greedy fashion, It's not my sins I'm worried about. So to Jesus' receding back, I had the gall to say "Am I also cured?"

He turned to face me, no sign of a smile, and finally said two words—"That too." Then he climbed from the water, not looking around, really done with me.

Greg Carey (b. 1965) is a New Testament professor and author of several books on the Gospels. He currently teaches at Lancaster Theological Seminary. This extract is taken from his Huffington Post blog, where he seeks to explain that Mark is deliberately mysterious about why the disciples follow Jesus, which, in contrast to John Grisham or Stieg Larsson or even the Gospel of Luke, is frustrating. Yet sometimes living with mystery is perhaps the only place we are allowed to be.

Biblical stories often frustrate us by refusing to provide all the details we desire. John Grisham would do better. If John Grisham had written Mark, we'd overhear a little dialogue between Simon and Andrew concerning Jesus. Stieg Larsson would have accompanied James and John through their morning routine. Patricia Cornwell would have clued us into the rumors that attend Jesus's arrival. Even the author of Luke's Gospel provides a little story that explains why the disciples find Jesus compelling. After a night of unsuccessful fishing, Simon, James and John allow Jesus to use their boat as a podium. Jesus tells the men to put out and fish again. Simon grumbles, but an overwhelming catch of fish convinces him that Jesus is the real deal (Luke 5:1-11). No wonder Simon and his colleagues leave everything to follow Jesus! But Mark remains reticent.

We should honor the Gospels' reticence. The Gospels will reward our patience by supplying occasional details. When we learn that Nicodemus comes to Jesus at night, but the Samaritan woman encounters him at noon, we know to pay attention (John 3:2; 4:6). After all, the Gospel tells us that to mind the distinction between those who love darkness and those who come to the light. Our ears likewise perk up when Jesus has the crowd recline on the green grass (Mark 6:39). "They were like sheep without a shepherd," Mark tells us (6:34), and we remember: "The LORD is my shepherd. . . . The LORD makes me lie down in green pastures" (Psalm 23:1-2). So when Mark refuses to tell us just why Simon and his colleagues abandon their former lives to follow Jesus, we hold our questions for later. But we do not forget them.

In Luke's Gospel, Jesus reads scripture and then announces that the scripture is fulfilled in the midst of the congregation. Martin Luther (1483-1586), in his famous *Table Talk* (conversations with the Doctor, where notes were taken) reflects on the significance and power of the text. Understanding scripture is hard, explains Luther, and to imagine that we have really understood the text is tantamount to claiming we are God.

> I call upon St. Peter, St. Paul, Moses, and all the Saints, to say whether they ever fundamentally comprehended one single word of God, without studying it over and over and over again. The Psalm says; *His understanding is infinite.* The saints, indeed, know God's Word, and can discourse of it, but the practice is another matter; therein we shall ever remain scholars.
>
> The school theologians have a fine similitude hereupon, that it is as with a sphere or globe, which, lying on a table, touches it only with one point, yet it is the whole table which supports the globe. Though I am an old doctor of divinity, to this day I have not got beyond the children's learning—the Ten Commandments, the Belief, and the Lord's Prayer; and these I understand not so well as I should, though I study them daily, praying, with my son John and my daughter Magdalene. If I thoroughly appreciated these first words of the Lord's Prayer, *Our Father, which art in Heaven,* and really believed that God, who made heaven and earth, and all creatures, and has all things in his hand, was my Father, then should I certainly conclude with myself, that I also am a lord of heaven and earth, that Christ is my brother, Gabriel

my servant, Raphael my coachman, and all the angels my attendants at need, given unto me by my heavenly Father, to keep me in the path, that unawares I knock not my foot against a stone. But that our faith may be exercised and confirmed, our heavenly Father suffers us to be cast into dungeons, or plunged in water. So we may see how finely we understand these words, and how belief shakes, and how great our weakness is, so that we begin to think—Ah, who knows how far that is true which is set forth in the scriptures?

XII.

No greater mischief can happen to a Christian people, than to have God's Word taken from them, or falsified, so that they no longer have it pure and clear. God grant we and our descendants be not witnesses of such a calamity.

XIII.

When we have God's Word pure and clear, then we think ourselves all right; we become negligent, and repose in a vain security; we no longer pay due heed, thinking it will always so remain; we do not watch and pray against the devil, who is ready to tear the Divine Word out of our hearts. It is with us as with travelers, who, so long as they are on the highway, are tranquil and heedless, but if they go astray into the woods or cross paths, uneasily seek which way to take, this or that.

XIV.

The great men and the doctors understand not the word of God, but it is revealed to the humble and to children, as it testified by the Saviour in the Gospel according to St Matthew, xi. 25: "O Father, Lord of heaven and earth, because thou hast hid these things from the wise and prudent, and hast revealed them unto babes." Gregory says, well and rightly, that the Holy Scripture is a stream of running water, where alike the elephant may swim, and the lamb walk without losing its feet.

XV.

The great unthankfulness, contempt of God's Word, and willfulness of the world, make me fear that the divine light will soon cease to shine on man, for God's Word has ever had its certain course.

In the time of kings of Judah, Baal obscured the brightness of God's Word, and it became hard labor to destroy his empire over the hearts of men. Even in the time of the apostles, there were heresies, errors, and evil doctrines spread abroad by false brethren. Next came Arius, and the Word of God was hidden behind dark clouds, but the holy fathers, Ambrose, Hilary, Augustine, Athanasius, and others, dispersed the obscurity. Greece and many other countries have heard the Word of God, but have since abandoned it, and it is to be feared even now it may quit Germany, and go into other lands. I hope the last day will not be long delayed. The darkness grows thicker around us, and godly servants of the Most High become rarer and more rare. Impiety and licentiousness are rampant throughout the world, and live like pigs, like wild beasts, devoid of all reason. But a voice will soon be heard thundering forth: *Behold, the bridegroom cometh.*

God will not be able to bear this wicked world much longer, but will come, with the dreadful day, and chastise the scorners of his word.

It is not about being rich and famous. It is not about being proud and strong. It is not about being a scribe or wearing a long robe or publishing many books. Jesus gets us. We are touched by a truly generous spirit. Wallace Stevens (1879-1955) spent most of his life working as an executive for an insurance company in Hartford, Connecticut. Thankfully, he also added to the canon of twentieth-century American Poetry. In this poem "Lebensweisheitspielerei," we see the complete touch captures a human life.

Weaker and weaker, the sunlight falls
In the afternoon, The proud and the strong
Have departed.

Those that are left are the unaccomplished.
The finally human.
Natives of a dwindled sphere.

Their indigence is an indigence
That is an indigence of the light,
A stellar pallor that hangs on the threads....

Each person completely touches us
With what he is and as he is,
In the stale grandeur of annihilation.

THE FOURTH SUNDAY AFTER THE EPIPHANY

Year A

Matthew 5:1-12

When Jesus saw the crowds, he went up the mountain; and after he sat down, his disciples came to him. Then he began to speak, and taught them, saying: "Blessed are the poor in spirit, for theirs is the kingdom of heaven. Blessed are those who mourn, for they will be comforted. Blessed are the meek, for they will inherit the earth. Blessed are those who hunger and thirst for righteousness, for they will be filled. Blessed are the merciful, for they will receive mercy. Blessed are the pure in heart, for they will see God. Blessed are the peacemakers, for they will be called children of God. Blessed are those who are persecuted for righteousness' sake, for theirs is the kingdom of heaven. Blessed are you when people revile you and persecute you and utter all kinds of evil against you falsely on my account. Rejoice and be glad, for your reward is great in heaven, for in the same way they persecuted the prophets who were before you."

Year B

Mark 1:21-28

Jesus and his disciples went to Capernaum; and when the Sabbath came, he entered the synagogue and taught. They were astounded at his teaching, for he taught them as one having authority, and not as the scribes. Just then there was in their synagogue a man with an unclean spirit, and he cried out, "What have you to do with us, Jesus of Nazareth? Have you come to destroy us? I know who you are, the Holy One of God." But Jesus rebuked him, saying, "Be silent, and come out of him!" And the unclean spirit, convulsing him and crying with a loud voice, came out of him. They were all amazed, and they kept on asking one another, "What is this? A new teaching—with authority! He commands even the unclean spirits, and they obey him." At once his fame began to spread throughout the surrounding region of Galilee.

Year C

Luke 4:21-30

In the synagogue at Nazareth, Jesus read from the book of the prophet Isaiah, and began to say, "Today this scripture has been fulfilled in your hearing." All spoke well of him and were amazed at the gracious words that came from his mouth. They said, "Is not this Joseph's son?" He said to them, "Doubtless you will quote to me this proverb, 'Doctor, cure yourself!' And you will say, 'Do here also in your hometown the things that we have heard you did at Capernaum.'" And he said, "Truly I tell you, no prophet is accepted in the prophet's hometown. But the truth is, there were many widows in Israel in the time of Elijah, when the heaven was shut up three years and six months, and there was a severe famine over all the land; yet Elijah was sent to none of them except to a widow at Zarephath in Sidon. There were also many lepers in Israel in the time of the prophet Elisha, and none of them was cleansed except Naaman the Syrian." When they heard this, all in the synagogue were filled with rage. They got up, drove him out of the town, and led him to the brow of the hill on which their town was built, so that they might hurl him off the cliff. But he passed through the midst of them and went on his way.

The Beatitudes in Matthew's gospel challenge us to go deeper into a life in Christ. For some in Jesus's time, just as they do today to some degree, these words signified a major upheaval and a threat to common thinking. This notion is picked up in a marvelous black-and-white film from director Pier Paolo Pasolini, *The Gospel According to Matthew* (1964). The sequence of the Sermon on the Mount is delivered in a fascinating way: the actor playing Christ is shot with dramatic close-ups, lighting effects, and through many different weather patterns. The effect is startling—and emphasizes the energy and potency of the words that Jesus is saying in Matthew's Gospel.

Henry Wadsworth Longfellow (1807-1882) was an American educator and poet. His distinguished career included teaching at Harvard College; and during his lifetime, he was probably the most popular poet in America. "The Song of Hiawatha" is a poem which weaves together Christian and Native American narratives. The poem tells the story of the Master of Life, Gitche Manito, who instructs the people of the earth to live in peace and promises a prophet will arise. Hiawatha is the son of Wenonah and grows into a wise visionary who embarks on various heroic deeds. This excerpt is from the second half of the poem, where Hiawatha is battling Pau-Puk-Keewis.

> In those days the Evil Spirits,
> All the Manitos of mischief,
> Fearing Hiawatha's wisdom,
> And his love for Chibiabos,
> Jealous of their faithful friendship,
> And their noble words and actions,
> Made at length a league against them,
> To molest them and destroy them.
> Hiawatha, wise and wary,
> Often said to Chibiabos,
> "O my brother! do not leave me,
> Lest the Evil Spirits harm you!"

In Luke, Jesus reads a passage from Isaiah and affirms that "Today this scripture has been affirmed in your hearing." Howard Thurman (1899-1981) was a major voice in the civil rights movement. Here in his book, *Jesus and the Disinherited*, Thurman reflects on Jesus the marginalized—a Jew under an occupying power—and how Jesus copes with fear. In this extract, he explains that one of the aspects of Jesus's response is to recognize his call and his own self-confident assertion of his identity.

It is instructive to inquire into the effects of fear on the disadvantaged. Fear becomes acute, in the form of panic or rage, only at the moment when what has been threat becomes actual violence; but the mere anticipation of such an encounter is overwhelming simply because the odds are basically uneven. This fact is important to hold in mind. The disadvantaged man knows that in any conflict he must deal not only with the particular individual involved but also with the entire group, then or later. Even recourse to the arbitration of law tends to be avoided because of the fear that the interpretations of law will be biased on the side of the dominant group. The result is the dodging of all encounters. The effect is nothing short of disaster in the organism; for, studies show, fear actually causes chemical changes in the body, affecting the blood stream and the muscular reactions, preparing the body either for fight or for flight. If flight is resorted to, it merely serves as an incentive to one's opponent to track down and overpower. Furthermore, not to fight back at the moment of descending violence is to be a coward, and to be deeply and profoundly humiliated in one's own estimation and in that of one's friends and family. If he is a man, he stands in the presence of his woman as not a man. While it may be true that many have not had such experiences, yet each stands in candidacy for such an experience. It is clear, then, that this fear, which served originally as a safety device, a kind of protective mechanism for the weak, finally becomes death for the self. The power that saves turns executioner. Within the walls of separateness death keeps watch. There are some who defer this death by yielding all claim to personal significance beyond the little world in which they live. In the absence of all hope ambition dies, and the very self is weakened, corroded. There remains only the elemental will to live and to accept life on the terms that are available. There is a profound measure of resourcefulness in all life, a resourcefulness that is guaranteed by the underlying aliveness of life itself. ...

Again the crucial question: Is there any help to be found for the disinherited in the religion of Jesus? Did Jesus deal with this kind of fear? If so, how did he do it? It is not merely, What did he say? even though his words are the important clues available to us. An analysis of the teaching of Jesus reveals that there is much that deals with the problems created by fear. After his temptation in the wilderness Jesus appeared in the synagogue and was asked to read the lesson. He chose to read from the prophet Isaiah the words which he declared as his fulfillment: The Spirit of the Lord is upon me, because he hath anointed me . . . to preach deliverance to the captives, and recovering of sight to the blind, to set at liberty them that are bruised, to preach the acceptable year of the Lord. And he closed the book . . . And he began to say unto them, This day is this scripture fulfilled in your ears. . . .

In this world the socially disadvantaged man is constantly given a negative answer to the most important personal questions upon which mental health depends: "Who am I? What am I?" The first question has to do with a basic self-estimate, a profound sense of belonging, of counting. If a man feels that he does not belong in the way in which it is perfectly normal for other people to belong, then he develops a deep sense of insecurity. When this happens to a person, it provides the basic material for what the psychologist calls an inferiority complex. It is quite possible for a man to have no sense of personal inferiority as such, but at the same time to be dogged by a sense of social inferiority. The awareness of being a child of God tends to stabilize the ego and results in a new courage, fearlessness, and power.

In *The Exorcist* (1973), young Regan MacNeil (Linda Blair) becomes possessed by a demon, held captive in her Georgetown apartment bedroom as her frantic mother (Ellen Burstyn) searches for any kind of deliverance. Based on the book by William Peter Blatty, *The Exorcist* also tells the story of two Jesuit priests who aid the possessed child: Fathers Lankester Merrin and Damien Karras—who not only must confront the unclean spirit in the child but also must confront their own personal demons that haunt them. In an echo of the confrontations Jesus has with demons in the Gospels, Father Merrin explains to Father Karras that the demon in Regan is ruthless and full of lies and deceit. In a haunting turn, Karras's own troubled past is used against him in a struggle with the evil force.

THE FIFTH SUNDAY
AFTER THE EPIPHANY

Year A

Matthew 5:13-20

Jesus said, "You are the salt of the earth; but if salt has lost its taste, how can its saltiness be restored? It is no longer good for anything, but is thrown out and trampled underfoot. "You are the light of the world. A city built on a hill cannot be hid. No one after lighting a lamp puts it under the bushel basket, but on the lampstand, and it gives light to all in the house. In the same way, let your light shine before others, so that they may see your good works and give glory to your Father in heaven. "Do not think that I have come to abolish the law or the prophets; I have come not to abolish but to fulfill. For truly I tell you, until heaven and earth pass away, not one letter, not one stroke of a letter, will pass from the law until all is accomplished. Therefore, whoever breaks one of the least of these commandments, and teaches others to do the same, will be called least in the kingdom of heaven; but whoever does them and teaches them will be called great in the kingdom of heaven. For I tell you, unless your righteousness exceeds that of the scribes and Pharisees, you will never enter the kingdom of heaven."

Year B

Mark 1:29-39

After Jesus and his disciples left the synagogue, they entered the house of Simon and Andrew, with James and John. Now Simon's mother-in-law was in bed with a fever, and they told him about her at once. He came and took her by the hand and lifted her up. Then the fever left her, and she began to serve them. That evening, at sundown, they brought to him all who were sick or possessed with demons. And the whole city was gathered around the door. And he cured many who were sick with various diseases, and cast out many demons; and he would not permit the demons to speak, because they knew him. In the morning, while it was still very dark, he got up and went out to a deserted place, and there he prayed. And Simon and his companions hunted for him. When they found him, they said to him, "Everyone is searching for you." He answered, "Let us go on to the neighboring towns, so that I may proclaim the message there also; for that is what I came out to do." And he went throughout Galilee, proclaiming the message in their synagogues and casting out demons.

Year C

Luke 5:1-11

Once while Jesus was standing beside the lake of Gennesaret, and the crowd was pressing in on him to hear the word of God, he saw two boats there at the shore of the lake; the fishermen had gone out of them and were washing their nets. He got into one of the boats, the one belonging to Simon, and asked him to put out a little way from the shore. Then he sat down and taught the crowds from the boat. When he had finished speaking, he said to Simon, "Put out into the deep water and let down your nets for a catch." Simon answered, "Master, we have worked all night long but have caught nothing. Yet if you say so, I will let down the nets." When they had done this, they caught so many fish that their nets were beginning to break. So they signaled their partners in the other boat to come and help them. And they came and filled both boats, so that they began to sink. But when Simon Peter saw it, he fell down at Jesus' knees, saying, "Go away from me, Lord, for I am a sinful man!" For he and all who were with him were amazed at the catch of fish that they had taken; and so also were James and John, sons of Zebedee, who were partners with Simon. Then Jesus said to Simon, "Do not be afraid; from now on you will be catching people." When they had brought their boats to shore, they left everything and followed him.

In Matthew, Jesus explains that the disciples are the salt of the earth. Ricardo Eliecer Neftali Reyes Basoalto (1904-1973), who wrote under a pen name Pablo Neruda, was a diplomat, politician, and poet from Chile. In "Ode to Salt," we have this powerful reflection on the significance and importance of salt.

I saw the salt
in this shaker
in the salt flats.
I know
you
will never believe me,
but
it sings,
through a mouth smothered
by earth.
I shuddered in those deep
Solitudes
when I heard
the voice
of
the salt in the desert.
Near Antofagasta
the entire
salt plain
speaks:
it is a
broken
voice,

A song full
of grief.
Then in its own mines
rock salt, a mountain
of buried light,
a cathedral through which light passes,
crystal of the sea, abandoned
by the waves.

And then on every table
on this earth,
salt,
your nimble
body
pouring out
the vigorous light
over
our foods.
Preserver
of the stores
of the ancient ships,
you were an explorer
in the ocean,
substance
going first
over the unknown, barely open
routes of the sea foam.
Dust of the sea, the tongue
receives a kiss
of the night from you:

taste recognizes
the ocean in each salted morsel,
and therefore the smallest,
the tiniest
wave of the shaker
brings home to us
not only your domestic whiteness
but the inward flavor
of the infinite.

Translation by Robert Bly

Mark's Gospel not only addresses the healing miracles of Jesus, such as in the healing of Simon Peter's mother-in-law, but also the ability to cast out demons. In Stephen King's (b. 1947) anthology series, *The Green Mile*, wrongly imprisoned John Coffey is a towering, simple man who has a miraculous ability to take away people's illnesses and pain. His prison guard Paul Edgecomb, who narrates the story, realizes Coffey may be able to "exorcise" his troubled warden's possessed, sickly wife. As a result, Paul begins to hatch a plan—and, in turn, begins to process this miraculous ability in terms of his own complicated faith beliefs.

I helped, didn't I?

Except *he* hadn't. *God* had. John Coffey's use of "I" could be chalked up to ignorance rather than pride, but I knew—believed, at least—what I had learned about healing in those churches of Praise Jesus, The Lord Is Mighty, piney-woods amen corners much beloved by my twenty-two-year-old mother and my aunts: that healing is never about the healed or the healer, but about God's will. For one to rejoice at the sick made well is normal, quite the expected thing, but the person healed has an obligation to then ask why—to meditate on God's will, and the extraordinary lengths to which God has gone to realize His will.

Peter, in Luke's narrative, finds himself unworthy in the presence of the sheer authority and power of Jesus. At this point, we are seeing the seed of worship. This sense will slowly grow into worshipping Jesus. William Temple (1881-1944), the Archbishop of Canterbury and scholar, writes movingly about the significance of worship.

> The fundamental business of life is always worship. At the root of all your being, your intellectual studies, the games you play, whatever it is, the impulse to do them well is and ought to be understood as being an impulse towards God, the source of all that is excellent. All life ought to be worship; and we know quite well there is no chance it will be worship unless we have times when we have worship and nothing else. No doubt when we are perfect, when fellowship with God is a constant realisation and joy, we shall not have to go backwards and forwards between times of worship and of the activities in which we show forth our loyalty to God; but we must do so now. Otherwise our interests in the world will cease for us to have any connection with God. It is our duty for a great part of the day to forget God, because if we are thinking about Him we shall not be thinking wholeheartedly about our duty in the world. Our duty to God requires that we should, for a good part of our time, be not consciously thinking about Him. That makes it absolutely necessary, if our life is to be a life of fellowship with Him, that we should have our times which are worship, pure and simple.
>
> The test of these is whether, as a result of them, we have more love for our fellow men.

The poem "The Coming" by R.S. Thomas (1913-2000) begins with a world literally held in the palm of God's hand—a world rife with struggle and pain. Rivers are serpentine and slimy, trees are bare, and the people are hungry. His "vanished April" signals a spring that seems to have never arrived—like the utter misery of the world into which Jesus finds himself in Mark's gospel: demons and evil and the people searching and reaching for a savior. It is all the more astounding that the "son" sees all of this and still says, "Let me go there."

> And God held in his hand
> A small globe. Look, he said.
> The son looked. Far off,
> As through water, he saw
> A scorched land of fierce
> Colour. The light burned
> There; crusted buildings
> Cast their shadows: a bright
> Serpent, a river
> Uncoiled itself, radiant
> With slime.
> On a bare
> Hill a bare tree saddened
> The Sky. Many people
> Held out their thin arms
> To it, as though waiting
> For a vanished April
> To return to its crossed
> Boughs. The son watched
> Them. Let me go there, he said.

THE SIXTH SUNDAY AFTER THE EPIPHANY

Year A

Matthew 5:21-37

Jesus said, "You have heard that it was said to those of ancient times, 'You shall not murder'; and 'whoever murders shall be liable to judgment.' But I say to you that if you are angry with a brother or sister, you will be liable to judgment; and if you insult a brother or sister, you will be liable to the council; and if you say, 'You fool,' you will be liable to the hell of fire. So when you are offering your gift at the altar, if you remember that your brother or sister has something against you, leave your gift there before the altar and go; first be reconciled to your brother or sister, and then come and offer your gift. Come to terms quickly with your accuser while you are on the way to court with him, or your accuser may hand you over to the judge, and the judge to the guard, and you will be thrown into prison. Truly I tell you, you will never get out until you have paid the last penny. "You have heard that it was said, 'You shall not commit adultery.' But I say to you that everyone who looks at a woman with lust has already committed adultery with her in his heart. If your right eye causes you to sin, tear it out and throw it away; it is better for you to lose one of your members than for your whole body to be thrown into hell. And if your right hand causes you to sin, cut it off and throw it away; it is better for you to lose one of your members than for your whole body to go into hell. "It was also said, 'Whoever divorces his wife, let him give her a certificate of divorce.' But I say to you that anyone who divorces his wife, except on the ground of unchastity, causes her to commit adultery; and whoever marries a divorced woman commits adultery. "Again, you have heard that it was said to those of ancient times, 'You shall not swear falsely, but carry out the vows you have made to the Lord.' But I say to you, Do not swear at all, either by heaven, for it is the throne of God, or by the earth, for it is his footstool, or by Jerusalem, for it is the city of the great King. And do not swear by your head, for you cannot make one hair white or black. Let your word be 'Yes, Yes' or 'No, No'; anything more than this comes from the evil one."

Year B

Mark 1:40-45

A leper came to Jesus begging him, and kneeling he said to him, "If you choose, you can make me clean." Moved with pity, Jesus stretched out his hand and touched him, and said to him, "I do choose. Be made clean!" Immediately the leprosy left him, and he was made clean. After sternly warning him he sent him away at once, saying to him, "See that you say nothing to anyone; but go, show yourself to the priest, and offer for your cleansing what Moses commanded, as a testimony to them." But he went out and began to proclaim it freely, and to spread the word, so that Jesus could no longer go into a town openly, but stayed out in the country; and people came to him from every quarter.

Year C

Luke 6:17-26

Jesus came down with the twelve apostles and stood on a level place, with a great crowd of his disciples and a great multitude of people from all Judea, Jerusalem, and the coast of Tyre and Sidon. They had come to hear him and to be healed of their diseases; and those who were troubled with unclean spirits were cured. And all in the crowd were trying to touch him, for power came out from him and healed all of them. Then he looked up at his disciples and said: "Blessed are you who are poor, for yours is the kingdom of God. Blessed are you who are hungry now, for you will be filled. Blessed are you who weep now, for you will laugh. Blessed are you when people hate you, and when they exclude you, revile you, and defame you on account of the Son of Man. Rejoice in that day and leap for joy, for surely your reward is great in heaven; for that is what their ancestors did to the prophets. But woe to you who are rich, for you have received your consolation. Woe to you who are full now, for you will be hungry. Woe to you who are laughing now, for you will mourn and weep. Woe to you when all speak well of you, for that is what their ancestors did to the false prophets."

In Matthew's Gospel, Jesus makes clear that there are consequences to our actions. Living life is about making decisions daily. The need to decide is also found in James 5:12: "But above all things, my brothers, swear not, neither by heaven, neither by the earth, neither by any other oath: but let your yes be yes; and your no, no; lest you fall into condemnation." In *Markings*, **Dag Hammarskjöld** (1905-1961) wrestled with the yes/no, either/or in life. His life was as a thoughtful civil servant, the Secretary-General of the United Nations.

> You cannot play with the animal in you without becoming wholly animal, play with falsehood without forfeiting your right to truth, play with cruelty without losing your sensitivity of mind. He who wants to keep his garden tidy does not reserve a plot for weeds.
>
> For all that has been,
> Thank you.
> For all that is to come,
> Yes!

In Mark's Gospel, we have the healing of the leper. John Newton (1725-1807) is best known for the hymn "Amazing Grace." He was a captain of slave ships. In this delightful poem, Newton enters imaginatively into the healing of the Leper, drawing the parallel between leprosy and sin and welcoming Christ to be the healer.

Oft as the leper's case I read,
My own described I feel;
Sin is a leprosy indeed.
Which none but Christ can heal.

Awhile I would have passed for well,
And strove my spots to hide;
Till it broke out incurable,
Too plain to be denied.

Then from the saints I sought to flee.
And dreaded to be seen;
I thought they all would point to me,
And cry, Unclean, unclean!

What anguish did my soul endure,
Till hope and patience ceased?
The more I strove myself to cure,
The more the plaque increased.

While thus I lay distressed, I saw
The Savior passing by;
To him, though filled with shame and awe,
I raised by mournful cry.

Lord, thou canst heal me if thou wilt,
For thou canst all things do;
O cleanse my leprous soul from guilt,
My filthy heart renew!

He heard, and with a gracious look,
Pronounced the healing word;
I will, be clean—and while he spoke
I felt my health restored.

Come lepers, seize the present hour,
The Saviour's grace to prove;
He can relieve, for his is pow'r,
He will, for he is love.

Luke's Sermon on the Plain is clearly focused on social justice. The "woe" sayings are brutal in their judgment. Sor Juana Ines de la Cruz (1648-1694) was a Mexican nun who captured that tone of judgment. During the colonial period, she wrote poems, plays, letters, and other works as well as writing music and doing scientific experiments. Her works were popular both in Mexico and Spain. Betrayed by a supposed friend for advocating for women's rights and education, she was silenced by the archbishop of Mexico. She remained faithful to her vocation to the end, dying while caring for others during a plague. "Hombres Necios" criticizes men who blame women for their own sins, holding them to account for their falsely justified transgressions.

> Silly, you men—so very adept
> at wrongly faulting womankind,
> not seeing you're alone to blame
> for faults you plant in woman's mind.
>
> After you've won by urgent plea
> the right to tarnish her good name,
> you still expect her to behave—
> you, that coaxed her into shame.
>
> You batter her resistance down
> and then, all righteousness, proclaim
> that feminine frivolity,
> not your persistence, is to blame.
>
> When it comes to bravely posturing,
> your witlessness must take the prize:
> you're the child that makes a bogeyman,
> and then recoils in fear and cries.

Presumptuous beyond belief,
you'd have the woman you pursue
be Thais when you're courting her,
Lucretia once she falls to you.

For plain default of common sense,
could any action be so queer
as oneself to cloud the mirror,
then complain that it's not clear?

Whether you're favored or disdained,
nothing can leave you satisfied.
You whimper if you're turned away,
you sneer if you've been gratified.

With you, no woman can hope to score;
whichever way, she's bound to lose;
spurning you, she's ungrateful—
succumbing, you call her lewd.

Your folly is always the same:
you apply a single rule
to the one you accuse of looseness
and the one you brand as cruel.

What happy mean could there be
for the woman who catches your eye,
if, unresponsive, she offends,
yet whose complaisance you decry?

Still, whether it's torment or anger—
and both ways you've yourselves to blame—
God bless the woman who won't have you,
no matter how loud you complain.

It's your persistent entreaties
that change her from timid to bold.
Having made her thereby naughty,
you would have her good as gold.

So where does the greater guilt lie
for a passion that should not be:
with the man who pleads out of baseness
or the woman debased by his plea?

Or which is more to be blamed—
though both will have cause for chagrin:
the woman who sins for money
or the man who pays money to sin?

So why are you men all so stunned
at the thought you're all guilty alike?
Either like them for what you've made them
or make of them what you can like.

If you'd give up pursuing them,
you'd discover, without a doubt,
you've a stronger case to make
against those who seek you out.

I well know what powerful arms
you wield in pressing for evil:
your arrogance is allied
with the world, the flesh, and the devil!

For Mark, the leper was not able to keep quiet. Being cleansed by Jesus was not a quiet, peaceful moment at the altar rail in a beautiful church. The person being healed has his/her life transformed; a new birth of wholeness is not unlike a natural birth. Both involve pain, tears, even violence. A new birth or cleansing makes right the grotesque in life. This is not a neat project for the faint-hearted.

From *The Incarnational Art of Flannery O'Connor*, Christina Bieber Lake:

Rene Girard explains that the ancient narratives of Jonah and Oedipus tell the same story of a "sacrificial crisis." When Jonah is on the way to Tarshish to escape his calling to Nineveh, God sends a storm to the ship. Each man on board prays to his own god: the community is in religious disorder. Jonah knows his disobedience is the cause and tells the crewmen to cast him into the sea. They do so, appealing to Jonah's God, and the tempest stops. Thebes is in a similar crisis because of Oedipus's actions, and he must be exiled before Thebes can be redeemed. In both cases the community must be cleansed of its polluted being; in both cases an act of violence is necessary for the cleansing.

The city of Taulkinham in *Wise Blood* is in this kind of religious disorder, but Haze participates in it willingly. As a result, Taulkinham becomes increasingly monstrous because . . . in mythology there is no difference between the morally monstrous and the physically monstrous.

THE SEVENTH SUNDAY AFTER THE EPIPHANY

Year A

Matthew 5:38-48

Jesus said, "You have heard that it was said, 'An eye for an eye and a tooth for a tooth.' But I say to you, Do not resist an evildoer. But if anyone strikes you on the right cheek, turn the other also; and if anyone wants to sue you and take your coat, give your cloak as well; and if anyone forces you to go one mile, go also the second mile. Give to everyone who begs from you, and do not refuse anyone who wants to borrow from you.

"You have heard that it was said, 'You shall love your neighbor and hate your enemy.' But I say to you, Love your enemies and pray for those who persecute you, so that you may be children of your Father in heaven; for he makes his sun rise on the evil and on the good, and sends rain on the righteous and on the unrighteous. For if you love those who love you, what reward do you have? Do not even the tax collectors do the same? And if you greet only your brothers and sisters, what more are you doing than others? Do not even the Gentiles do the same? Be perfect, therefore, as your heavenly Father is perfect."

Year B

Mark 2:1-12

When Jesus returned to Capernaum after some days, it was reported that he was at home. So many gathered around that there was no longer room for them, not even in front of the door; and he was speaking the word to them. Then some people came, bringing to him a paralyzed man, carried by four of them. And when they could not bring him to Jesus because of the crowd, they removed the roof above him; and after having dug through it, they let down the mat on which the paralytic lay. When Jesus saw their faith, he said to the paralytic, "Son, your sins are forgiven." Now some of the scribes were sitting there, questioning in their hearts, "Why does this fellow speak in this way? It is blasphemy! Who can forgive sins but God alone?" At once Jesus perceived in his spirit that they were discussing these questions among themselves; and he said to them, "Why do you raise such questions in your hearts? Which is easier, to say to the paralytic, 'Your sins are forgiven,' or to say, 'Stand up and take your mat and walk'? But so that you may know that the Son of Man has authority on earth to forgive sins"—he said to the paralytic—"I say to you, stand up, take your mat and go to your home." And he stood up, and immediately took the mat and went out before all of them; so that they were all amazed and glorified God, saying, "We have never seen anything like this!"

Year C

Luke 6:27-38

Jesus said, "I say to you that listen, Love your enemies, do good to those who hate you, bless those who curse you, pray for those who abuse you. If anyone strikes you on the cheek, offer the other also; and from anyone who takes away your coat do not withhold even your shirt. Give to everyone who begs from you; and if anyone takes away your goods, do not ask for them again. Do to others as you would have them do to you. If you love those who love you, what credit is that to you? For even sinners love those who love them. If you do good to those who do good to you, what credit is that to you? For even sinners do the same. If you lend to those from whom you hope to receive, what credit is that to you? Even sinners lend to sinners, to receive as much again. But love your enemies, do good, and lend, expecting nothing in return. Your reward will be great, and you will be children of the Most High; for he is kind to the ungrateful and the wicked. Be merciful, just as your Father is merciful. Do not judge, and you will not be judged; do not condemn, and you will not be condemned. Forgive, and you will be forgiven; give, and it will be given to you. A good measure, pressed down, shaken together, running over, will be put into your lap; for the measure you give will be the measure you get back."

In the sermon on the Mount, we find Jesus advocating non-violence. Walter Wink (1935-2012) developed one of the most famous defenses of non-violence as advocated in the teaching of Jesus. This extract invites Christians to be faithful to the teaching of Jesus and oppose our propensities to violence.

Many otherwise devout Christians simply dismiss Jesus's teachings about nonviolence out of hand as impractical idealism. And with good reason. "Turn the other cheek" has come to imply a passive, doormat-like quality that has made the Christian way seem cowardly and complicit in the face of injustice. "Resist not evil" seems to break the back of all opposition to evil and to counsel submission. "Going the second mile" has become a platitude meaning nothing more than "extend yourself" and appears to encourage collaboration with the oppressor. Jesus's teaching, viewed this way, is impractical, masochistic, and even suicidal—an invitation to bullies and spouse-batterers to wipe up the floor with their supine Christian victims.

Jesus never displayed that kind of passivity. Whatever the source of the misunderstanding, such distortions are clearly neither in Jesus nor his teaching, which, in context, is one of the most revolutionary political statements ever uttered:

You have heard that it was said, "An eye for an eye and a tooth for a tooth." But I say to you, Do not resist an evildoer. But if anyone strikes you on the right cheek, turn the other also; and if anyone wants to sue you and take your coat, give your cloak as well; and if anyone forces you to go one mile, go also the second mile (Matt. 5:38-41; see also Luke 6:29).

The traditional interpretation of "do not resist an evildoer" has been nonresistance to evil—an odd conclusion, given the fact that on every occasion Jesus himself resisted evil with every fiber of his being. The fifth-century theologian Augustine agreed that the gospel teaches nonresistance, and therefore declared that a Christian must not attempt self-defense. However, he noted, if someone is attacking my neighbor, then the love commandment requires me to defend my neighbor, by force of arms if necessary. With that deft stroke, Augustine opened the door to the just-war theory, the military defense of the Roman Empire, and the use of torture and capital punishment. Following his lead, Christians have ever since been justifying wars fought for nothing more than national interest as "just."

Curiously enough, some pacifists have also bought the nonresistance interpretation, and therefore have rejected nonviolent direct action and civil disobedience as coercive and in violation of the law of Christ.

But the gospel does not teach nonresistance to evil. Jesus counsels resistance, but without violence. The Greek word translated "resist" in Matt. 5:39 is antistenai, meaning literally to stand (stenai) against (anti). What translators have over-looked is that antistenai is most often used in the Greek version of the Old Testament as a technical term for warfare. It describes the way opposing armies would march toward each other until their ranks met. Then they would "take a stand," that is, fight. Ephesians 6:13 uses precisely this imagery: "Therefore take up the whole armor of God, so that you may be able to withstand [antistenai] on that evil day, and having done everything, to stand firm istenai]." The image is not of a punch-drunk boxer somehow managing to stay on his feet, but of soldiers standing their ground, refusing to flee. In short, anti-stenai means more here than simply to "resist" evil. It means to resist violently, to revolt or rebel, to engage in an armed insurrection.

The Bible translators working in the hire of King James on what came to be known as the King James Version knew that the king did not want people to conclude that they had any recourse against his or any other sovereign's tyranny. James had explicitly commissioned a new translation of the Bible because of what he regarded as "seditious . . . dangerous, and trayterous" tendencies in the marginal notes printed in the Geneva Bible, which included endorsement of the right to disobey a tyrant. Therefore the public had to be made to believe that there are two alternatives, and only two: flight or fight. And Jesus is made to command us, according to these king's men, to resist not. Jesus appears to authorize monarchical absolutism. Submission is the will of God. And most modern translators have meekly followed in that path.

Jesus is not telling us to submit to evil, but to refuse to oppose it on its own terms. We are not to let the opponent dictate the methods of our opposition. He is urging us to transcend both passivity and violence by finding a third way, one that is at once assertive and yet nonviolent. The correct translation would be the one still preserved in the earliest renditions of this saying found in the New Testament epistles: "Do not repay evil for evil" (Rom. 12:17; 1 Thes. 5:15; 1 Pet. 3:9). The Scholars Version of Matt. 5:39a is superb: "Don't react violently against the one who is evil."

Explicitly in Mark, but also in the opening obligation of Matthew and Luke to love our enemies, we find that forgiveness is central to the gospel. It is a radical way of coming to terms with the past. Both forgiving and being forgiven are vital ways of helping us live into the future without the past haunting us. *The Invention of Wings* by Sue Monk Kidd (b. 1948) is a powerful, imaginative retelling of the moving story of two sisters, who grew up in Charleston, South Carolina, in the early nineteenth century, and became powerful advocates for both the abolition of slavery and for feminism. In this extract, Sarah is with her father as he is about to die. The theme of forgiveness comes to the fore as he seeks his daughter's forgiveness for the many moments when he tried to crush his daughter's spirit. The extract starts with the father explaining that he has not got long to go.

"Sarah. My dear girl. Let's not indulge vain hopes. I don't expect to recover, nor do I want to."

His face blazed intensely now. I took his hand and gradually his expression eased, and he drifted to sleep.

He woke at three in the afternoon. The white flag had just been raised—I could see it framed in the window, snapping against the translucent sky. I held the water glass to his lips and helped him to drink. He said, "We've had our quarrels, haven't we?"

I knew what was coming and I wanted to spare him. To spare me. "It doesn't matter now."

"You've always had a strong, separate mind, perhaps even a radical mind, and I was harsh with you at times. You must forgive me."

I couldn't imagine what it cost him to say these words. "I do," I said. "And you must forgive me."

"Forgive you for what, Sarah? For following your conscience? Do you think I don't abhor slavery as you do? Do you think I don't know it was greed that kept me from following my conscience as you have? The plantation, the house, our entire way of life depended on the slave." His face contorted and he clutched at his side a moment before going on. "Or should I forgive you for wanting to give natural expression to your intellect? You were smarter than even Thomas or John, but you're female, another cruelty I was helpless to change."

"Father, please. I have no resentment of you." It wasn't completely true, but I said it.

In Matthew and Luke, we are exhorted to love our neighbor. But what exactly does that mean? In this short story by Raymond Carver (1938-1998) called "A Small Good Thing," a baker ends up making the difference. The baker offers his "warm cinnamon buns" to grieving parents just as a priest offers the bread and wine to the faithful. The act of gratitude and sharing is healing and reconciling. There is forgiveness in the sharing of "a small good thing."

It was warm inside the bakery. Howard stood up from the table and took off his coat. He helped Ann from her coat. The baker looked at them for a minute and then nodded and got up from the table. He went to the oven and turned off some switches. He found cups and poured coffee from an electric coffee-maker. He put a carton of cream on the table, and a bowl of sugar.

"You probably need to eat something," the baker said. "I hope you'll eat some of my hot rolls. You have to eat and keep going. Eating is a small, good thing in a time like this," he said.

He served them warm cinnamon rolls just out of the oven, the icing still runny. He put butter on the table and knives to spread the butter. Then the baker sat down at the table with them. He waited. He waited until they each took a roll from the platter and began to eat. "It's good to eat something," he said, watching them. "There's more. Eat up. Eat all you want. There's all the rolls in the world in here."

They ate rolls and drank coffee. Ann was suddenly hungry, and the rolls were warm and sweet. She ate three of them, which pleased the baker. Then he began to talk. They listened carefully. Although they were tired and in anguish, they listened to what the baker had to say. They nodded when the baker began to speak of loneliness, and of the sense of doubt and limitation that had come to him in his middle years. He told them what it was like to be childless all these years. To repeat the days with the ovens endlessly full and endlessly empty. The party food, the celebrations he'd worked over. Icing knuckle-deep. The tiny wedding couples stuck into cakes. Hundreds of them, no, thousands by now. Birthdays. Just imagine all those candles burning. He had a necessary trade. He was a baker. He was glad he wasn't a florist. It was better to be feeding people. This was a better smell anytime than flowers.

"Smell this," the baker said, breaking open a dark loaf. "It's a heavy bread, but rich." They smelled it, then he had them taste it. It had the taste of molasses and coarse grains. They listened to him. They ate what they could. They swallowed the dark bread. It was like daylight under the fluorescent trays of light. They talked on into the early morning, the high, pale cast of light in the windows, and they did not think of leaving.

Carnivàle (2003-2005) was a fantastical series that juggled large theological themes and allegories while still providing thrills, suspense, and HBO's patented mature drama. For two seasons, viewers were treated to a most unusual story of a Dust Bowl-era traveling circus troupe. The opus centered on a struggle of good and evil embodied in a corrupt, evil priest (Clancy Brown) plotting a revolution in California and his counterpart—a young troubled man named Ben Hawkins (Nick Stahl), who has the gift of healing. When Hawkins temporarily takes up residence with the "carnies," they soon begin to witness his abilities—and seek to exploit this miracle worker.

THE EIGHTH SUNDAY
AFTER THE EPIPHANY

Year A

Matthew 6:24-34

Jesus said, "No one can serve two masters; for a slave will either hate the one and love the other, or be devoted to the one and despise the other. You cannot serve God and wealth. "Therefore I tell you, do not worry about your life, what you will eat or what you will drink, or about your body, what you will wear. Is not life more than food, and the body more than clothing? Look at the birds of the air; they neither sow nor reap nor gather into barns, and yet your heavenly Father feeds them. Are you not of more value than they? And can any of you by worrying add a single hour to your span of life? And why do you worry about clothing? Consider the lilies of the field, how they grow; they neither toil nor spin, yet I tell you, even Solomon in all his glory was not clothed like one of these. But if God so clothes the grass of the field, which is alive today and tomorrow is thrown into the oven, will he not much more clothe you—you of little faith? Therefore do not worry, saying, 'What will we eat?' or 'What will we drink?' or 'What will we wear?' For it is the Gentiles who strive for all these things; and indeed your heavenly Father knows that you need all these things. But strive first for the kingdom of God and his righteousness, and all these things will be given to you as well. "So do not worry about tomorrow, for tomorrow will bring worries of its own. Today's trouble is enough for today."

Year B

Mark 2:13-22

Jesus went out again beside the sea; the whole crowd gathered around him, and he taught them. As he was walking along, he saw Levi son of Alphaeus sitting at the tax booth, and he said to him, "Follow me." And he got up and followed him. And as he sat at dinner in Levi's house, many tax collectors and sinners were also sitting with Jesus and his disciples—for there were many who followed him. When the scribes of the Pharisees saw that he was eating with sinners and tax collectors, they said to his disciples, "Why does he eat with tax collectors and sinners?" When Jesus heard this, he said to them, "Those who are well have no need of a physician, but those who are sick; I have come to call not the righteous but sinners." Now John's disciples and the Pharisees were fasting; and people came and said to him, "Why do John's disciples and the disciples of the Pharisees fast, but your disciples do not fast?" Jesus said to them, "The wedding guests cannot fast while the bridegroom is with them, can they? As long as they have the bridegroom with them, they cannot fast. The days will come when the bridegroom is taken away from them, and then they will fast on that day. "No one sews a piece of unshrunk cloth on an old cloak; otherwise, the patch pulls away from it, the new from the old, and a worse tear is made. And no one puts new wine into old wineskins; otherwise, the wine will burst the skins, and the wine is lost, and so are the skins; but one puts new wine into fresh wineskins."

Year C

Luke 6:39-49

Jesus told the people a parable: "Can a blind person guide a blind person? Will not both fall into a pit? A disciple is not above the teacher, but everyone who is fully qualified will be like the teacher. Why do you see the speck in your neighbor's eye, but do not notice the log in your own eye? Or how can you say to your neighbor, 'Friend, let me take out the speck in your eye,' when you yourself do not see the log in your own eye? You hypocrite, first take the log out of your own eye, and then you will see clearly to take the speck out of your neighbor's eye. "No good tree bears bad fruit, nor again does a bad tree bear good fruit; for each tree is known by its own fruit. Figs are not gathered from thorns, nor are grapes picked from a bramble bush. The good person out of the good treasure of the heart produces good, and the evil person out of evil treasure produces evil; for it is out of the abundance of the heart that the mouth speaks. "Why do you call me 'Lord, Lord,' and do not do what I tell you? I will show you what someone is like who comes to me, hears my words, and acts on them. That one is like a man building a house, who dug deeply and laid the foundation on rock; when a flood arose, the river burst against that house but could not shake it, because it had been well built. But the one who hears and does not act is like a man who built a house on the ground without a foundation. When the river burst against it, immediately it fell, and great was the ruin of that house."

The injunction in Matthew 6 that we must not worry is one of the hardest of all of the commandments of Jesus to observe. Kathleen Jessie Raine (1908-2003) was a poet and scholar with a particular academic interest in William Blake and W. B. Yeats. She was a research fellow at Girton College, Cambridge. In this poem "Worry about Money," she muses on the advice from her bank manager and the advice she gets from the simple fact of "living." Do note how the last three lines are referring to 1 Kings 17:7-16.

Wearing worry about money like a hair shirt
I lie down in my bed and wrestle with my angel.

My bank-manager could not sanction my
    continuance for another day
But life itself wakes me each morning, and love

Urges me to give although I have no money
In the bank at this moment, and ought properly

To cease to exist in a world where poverty
Is a shameful and ridiculous offence.

Having no one to advise me, I open the Bible
And shut my eyes and put my finger on a text

And read that the widow with the young son
Must give first to the prophetic genius
From the little there is in the bin of flour and the
    cruse of oil.

The poem "New Wine" by Robert Maxwell Bartley (1878-1960) engages the text of Jesus's parable "new wine into old wineskins" head on, and indeed, engages the Lord in a debate about parable-making in general. What results is a brief but serious dialogue and push-back on the notion of metaphor and the theology of conversation with the Almighty.

> Never, no never put new wine into old bottles.
>> An adage in three books of the testament found.
> Advice is sweet to gumption with throttles!
>> Dear Saviour your parables are proverbially sound.
>
> Dear Saviour, methinks the Cosmic disaster is
>> Putting new wine
> Into old bottles with foretold results?
> Help us to touch that magic raiment of thine
>> And—hurry father-time to the ults.

For the Jesus of Luke's Gospel, good comes out of good people. This is a classic text for virtue ethics: it is who we are that matters. Emily Bronte (1818-1848), in *Wuthering Heights*, explores the complexity of human life and how muddled we all can be. Here Cathy is making the decision to marry Edgar Linton rather than her true love Heathcliff. She opts to be seen with the right person. In this extract she is in conversation with Nelly, the housekeeper.

> "Today, Edgar Linton has asked me to marry him, and I've given him an answer. — Now, before I tell you whether it was a consent, or denial — you tell me which it ought to have been."
>
> "Really, Miss Catherine, how can I know?" I replied. "To be sure, considering the exhibition you performed in his presence, this afternoon, I might say it would be wise to refuse him — since he asked you after that, he must either be hopelessly stupid, or a venturesome fool."
>
> "If you talk so, I won't tell you any more," she returned, peevishly, rising to her feet, "I accepted him, Nelly. Be quick, and say whether I was wrong!"
>
> *[After a protracted conversation about whether Cathy loves Edgar, Cathy finally confesses everything.]*.
>
> "This is nothing," cried she; "I was only going to say that heaven did not seem to be my home; and I broke my heart with weeping to come back to earth; and the angels were so angry that they flung me out, into the middle of the heath on the top of Wuthering Heights, where I woke sobbing for joy. That will do to explain my secret, as well as the other, I've no more business to marry Edgar Linton

than I have to be in heaven; and if the wicked man in there had not brought Heathcliff so low, I shouldn't have thought of it. It would degrade me to marry Heathcliff, now; so he shall never know how I love him; and that, not because he's handsome, Nelly, but because he's more myself than I am. Whatever our souls are made of, his and mine are the same, and Linton's is as different as a moonbeam from lightning, or frost from fire."

Ere this speech ended, I became sensible of Heathcliff's presence. Having noticed a slight movement, I turned my head, and saw him rise from the bench, and steal out, noiselessly. He had listened till he heard Catherine say it would degrade her to marry him, and then he stayed to hear no further.

———— ⚭ ————

The late singer-songwriter John Denver (1943-1997) was known for his ecological activism that burst forth from his country-pop ballads and standards such as "Rocky Mountain High" and "Country Roads (Take Me Home)." But he was a fine composer of love songs as well, and particularly ballads that transcended the typical "boy meets girl, girl meets boy" formula of the 1960s and early 1970s. The song, "Follow Me," echoes Christ's significant plea in this gospel lesson to turn and "follow" him. The lyrics capture the complex human engagement as one life seeks to impact another. The chorus of Denver's song particularly echoes the sentiments of the Marcan pericope as he implores the listener to "make it part of you to be a part of me."

LAST SUNDAY AFTER THE EPIPHANY

Year A

Matthew 17:1-9

Six days later, Jesus took with him Peter and James and his brother John and led them up a high mountain, by themselves. And he was transfigured before them, and his face shone like the sun, and his clothes became dazzling white. Suddenly there appeared to them Moses and Elijah, talking with him. Then Peter said to Jesus, "Lord, it is good for us to be here; if you wish, I will make three dwellings here, one for you, one for Moses, and one for Elijah." While he was still speaking, suddenly a bright cloud overshadowed them, and from the cloud a voice said, "This is my Son, the Beloved; with him I am well pleased; listen to him!" When the disciples heard this, they fell to the ground and were overcome by fear. But Jesus came and touched them, saying, "Get up and do not be afraid." And when they looked up, they saw no one except Jesus himself alone. As they were coming down the mountain, Jesus ordered them, "Tell no one about the vision until after the Son of Man has been raised from the dead."

Year B

Mark 9:2-9

Jesus took with him Peter and James and John, and led them up a high mountain apart, by themselves. And he was transfigured before them, and his clothes became dazzling white, such as no one on earth could bleach them. And there appeared to them Elijah with Moses, who were talking with Jesus. Then Peter said to Jesus, "Rabbi, it is good for us to be here; let us make three dwellings, one for you, one for Moses, and one for Elijah." He did not know what to say, for they were terrified. Then a cloud overshadowed them, and from the cloud there came a voice, "This is my Son, the Beloved; listen to him!" Suddenly when they looked around, they saw no one with them anymore, but only Jesus. As they were coming down the mountain, he ordered them to tell no one about what they had seen, until after the Son of Man had risen from the dead.

Year C

Luke 9:28-36, [37-43a]

About eight days after Peter had acknowledged Jesus as the Christ of God, Jesus took with him Peter and John and James, and went up on the mountain to pray. And while he was praying, the appearance of his face changed, and his clothes became dazzling white. Suddenly they saw two men, Moses and Elijah, talking to him. They appeared in glory and were speaking of his departure, which he was about to accomplish at Jerusalem. Now Peter and his companions were weighed down with sleep; but since they had stayed awake, they saw his glory and the two men who stood with him. Just as they were leaving him, Peter said to Jesus, "Master, it is good for us to be here; let us make three dwellings, one for you, one for Moses, and one for Elijah"—not knowing what he said. While he was saying this, a cloud came and overshadowed them; and they were terrified as they entered the cloud. Then from the cloud came a voice that said, "This is my Son, my Chosen; listen to him!" When the voice had spoken, Jesus was found alone. And they kept silent and in those days told no one any of the things they had seen. [On the next day, when they had come down from the mountain, a great crowd met him. Just then a man from the crowd shouted, "Teacher, I beg you to look at my son; he is my only child. Suddenly a spirit seizes him, and all at once he shrieks. It convulses him until he foams at the mouth; it mauls him and will scarcely leave him. I begged your disciples to cast it out, but they could not." Jesus answered, "You faithless and perverse generation, how much longer must I be with you and bear with you? Bring your son here." While he was coming, the demon dashed him to the ground in convulsions. But Jesus rebuked the unclean spirit, healed the boy, and gave him back to his father. And all were astounded at the greatness of God.]

Ayodeji Malcolm Guite (b. 1957) is a poet, priest, academic, and songwriter. In this poem, "Transfiguration," Guite captures the simplicity of the moment. Without fanfare, unlike Christmas, we simply see the "Love that dances at the heart of things."

> For that one moment, 'in and out of time',
> On that one mountain where all moments meet,
> The daily veil that covers the sublime
> In darkling glass fell dazzled at his feet.
> There were no angels full of eyes and wings
> Just living glory full of truth and grace.
> The Love that dances at the heart of things
> Shone out upon us from a human face
> And to that light the light in us leaped up,
> We felt it quicken somewhere deep within,
> A sudden blaze of long-extinguished hope
> Trembled and tingled through the tender skin.
> Nor can this this blackened sky, this darkened scar
> Eclipse that glimpse of how things really are.

Transfiguration is the moment when God is made visible and the significance of Jesus is seen. Making God visible is the theme of the reflections of John A.T. Robinson (1919-1983) on the death of a 16-year-old girl.

Two years ago I found myself having to speak at the funeral of a 16-year-old girl who died in our Yorkshire dale. I said stumblingly that God was to be found in the cancer as much as the sunset. That I firmly believed, but it was an intellectual statement. Now I have had to ask if I can say it of myself, which is a much greater test.

When I said it from the pulpit, I gather it produced quite a shock wave. I guess this was for two reasons.

1. Because I had mentioned the word openly in public—and even among Christians it is (or it was for much happened in the short time since) the great unmentionable. "Human kind," said Eliot, "cannot bear very much reality." . . .

2. The shock-wave was also no doubt due to my saying that God was in the cancer. As I made absolutely clear at the time, by this I did not mean that God was in it by intending or sending it. That would make him a very devil. Yet people always see these things in terms of his deliberate purpose or the failure of it. Why does he allow it? They say, and they get angry with God. Or rather, they project their anger on to God. And to let the anger come out is no bad thing. For so often diseases of strain and depression are caused by suppressed anger and hatred of other people or of

oneself. So it is healthy that it should come out—and God can take it . . . For God is to be found in cancer as in everything else. If he is not, then he is not the God of the Psalmist who said, "If I go down to hell, thou are there also," let alone of the Christian who knows God most deeply in the Cross.

Based on Victor Hugo's novel of the same name, *Les Misérablés* became a Broadway sensation when it debuted in 1985. Writers Alain Boubil and Jean-Marc Natel found a musical accessibility to a melodramatic storyline that struck a chord with audiences around the world. Of the many memorable songs in the opus, the Epilogue at the conclusion wraps up many various threads with a simple sentence—"to love another person is to see the face of God"—that harmonizes shockingly well with the impact of the Transfiguration event—truth revealed in the form of love.

At the Transfiguration, Peter and James experience a glimpse of the fullness of Christ's divinity. Jesus invites them to see this by asking them to climb a mountain. Eighteenth-century French Jesuit Jean Pierre de Caussade (1675-1751) reflected on how to encounter God and enter more fully into His presence in his poem, "The Divine Will."

> The divine will
> is a deep abyss
> of which the present
> moment is the entrance.
> If you plunge
> into this abyss
> you will find it
> infinitely more vast
> than your
> desires.

ASH WEDNESDAY

Year A, B, and C

Matthew 6:1-6, 16-21

Jesus said, "Beware of practicing your piety before others in order to be seen by them; for then you have no reward from your Father in heaven. "So whenever you give alms, do not sound a trumpet before you, as the hypocrites do in the synagogues and in the streets, so that they may be praised by others. Truly I tell you, they have received their reward. But when you give alms, do not let your left hand know what your right hand is doing, so that your alms may be done in secret; and your Father who sees in secret will reward you. "And whenever you pray, do not be like the hypocrites; for they love to stand and pray in the synagogues and at the street corners, so that they may be seen by others. Truly I tell you, they have received their reward. But whenever you pray, go into your room and shut the door and pray to your Father who is in secret; and your Father who sees in secret will reward you. "And whenever you fast, do not look dismal, like the hypocrites, for they disfigure their faces so as to show others that they are fasting. Truly I tell you, they have received their reward. But when you fast, put oil on your head and wash your face, so that your fasting may be seen not by others but by your Father who is in secret; and your Father who sees in secret will reward you. "Do not store up for yourselves treasures on earth, where moth and rust consume and where thieves break in and steal; but store up for yourselves treasures in heaven, where neither moth nor rust consumes and where thieves do not break in and steal. For where your treasure is, there your heart will be also."

The theme of authenticity is important. In *1984* by George Orwell (1903-1950), whose real name was Eric Arthur Blair, the human capacity to find self-interested reasons for inauthenticity is captured. In this extract, Winston and Julia muse on the systematic denial of truth by the Party.

In some ways she was far more acute than Winston, and far less susceptible to Party propaganda. Once when he happened in some connection to mention the war against Eurasia, she startled him by saying casually that in her opinion the war was not happening. The rocket bombs which fell daily on London were probably fired by the Government of Oceania itself, "just to keep people frightened." This was an idea that had literally never occurred to him. She also stirred a sort of envy in him by telling him that during the Two Minutes Hate her great difficulty was to avoid bursting out laughing. But she only questioned the teachings of the Party when they in some way touched upon her own life. Often she was ready to accept the official mythology, simply because the difference between truth and falsehood did not seem important to her. She believed, for instance, having learnt it at school, that the Party had invented aeroplanes . . . And when he told her that aeroplanes had been in existence before he was born, and long before the Revolution, the fact struck her as totally uninteresting. After all, what did it matter who had invented aeroplanes.

Elizabeth-Anne Stewart (b. 1951) is a Roman Catholic and spirituality educator. In this poem "Ashes," Stewart describes the link between last year's palms and the present moment of confession. The moment connects with the past and other recipients who are also confessing their sins.

You thumbed grit
Into my furrowed brow,
Marking me
With the sign of mortality,
The dust of last year's palms.
The cross you traced
Seared, smudged skin,
And I recalled
Other ashes
Etched
Into my heart
By those who love too little
Or not at all.

Thomas Stearns "T.S." Eliot (1888-1965) is considered one of the great poets of the twentieth century. American by birth, he spent most of his life in England. "Ash Wednesday" was written in 1930. It is known as Eliot's "conversion poem."

Because I do not hope to turn again
Because I do not hope
Because I do not hope to turn
Desiring this man's gift and that man's scope
I no longer strive to strive towards such things
(Why should the aged eagle stretch its wings?)
Why should I mourn
The vanished power of the usual reign?
Because I do not hope to know again
The infirm glory of the positive hour
Because I do not think
Because I know I shall not know
The one veritable transitory power
Because I cannot drink
There, where trees flower, and springs flow, for there is
nothing again
Because I know that time is always time
And place is always and only place
And what is actual is actual only for one time
And only for one place
I rejoice that things are as they are and
I renounce the blessed face
And renounce the voice
Because I cannot hope to turn again

Consequently I rejoice, having to construct something
Upon which to rejoice
And pray to God to have mercy upon us
And pray that I may forget
These matters that with myself I too much discuss
Too much explain
Because I do not hope to turn again
Let these words answer
For what is done, not to be done again
May the judgement not be too heavy upon us
Because these wings are no longer wings to fly
But merely vans to beat the air
The air which is now thoroughly small and dry
Smaller and dryer than the will
Teach us to care and not to care
Teach us to sit still.
Pray for us sinners now and at the hour of our death
Pray for us now and at the hour of our death.

Steven Spielberg's (b. 1946) acclaimed film, *Schindler's List* (1993, based on the book by Thomas Keneally), is built around the true story of Oskar Schindler who maneuvered to save thousands of lives of persecuted Jews in Poland during the height of the Holocaust. Before his heroic act, Schindler first must come to a place of recognizing the fragility of humanity and the threat of the Holocaust. A stirring visual sequence involves Schindler observing the effects of an incinerator—the soft snow of human ashes upon his clothes and his automobile.

THE FIRST SUNDAY IN LENT

Year A

Matthew 4:1-11

Jesus was led up by the Spirit into the wilderness to be tempted by the devil. He fasted forty days and forty nights, and afterwards he was famished. The tempter came and said to him, "If you are the Son of God, command these stones to become loaves of bread." But he answered, "It is written, 'One does not live by bread alone, but by every word that comes from the mouth of God.'" Then the devil took him to the holy city and placed him on the pinnacle of the temple, saying to him, "If you are the Son of God, throw yourself down; for it is written, 'He will command his angels concerning you,' and 'On their hands they will bear you up, so that you will not dash your foot against a stone.'" Jesus said to him, "Again it is written, 'Do not put the Lord your God to the test.'" Again, the devil took him to a very high mountain and showed him all the kingdoms of the world and their splendor; and he said to him, "All these I will give you, if you will fall down and worship me." Jesus said to him, "Away with you, Satan! for it is written, 'Worship the Lord your God, and serve only him.'" Then the devil left him, and suddenly angels came and waited on him.

Year B

Mark 1:9-15

In those days Jesus came from Nazareth of Galilee and was baptized by John in the Jordan. And just as he was coming up out of the water, he saw the heavens torn apart and the Spirit descending like a dove on him. And a voice came from heaven, "You are my Son, the Beloved; with you I am well pleased." And the Spirit immediately drove him out into the wilderness. He was in the wilderness forty days, tempted by Satan; and he was with the wild beasts; and the angels waited on him. Now after John was arrested, Jesus came to Galilee, proclaiming the good news of God, and saying, "The time is fulfilled, and the kingdom of God has come near; repent, and believe in the good news."

Year C

Luke 4:1-13

After his baptism, Jesus, full of the Holy Spirit, returned from the Jordan and was led by the Spirit in the wilderness, where for forty days he was tempted by the devil. He ate nothing at all during those days, and when they were over, he was famished. The devil said to him, "If you are the Son of God, command this stone to become a loaf of bread." Jesus answered him, "It is written, 'One does not live by bread alone.'" Then the devil led him up and showed him in an instant all the kingdoms of the world. And the devil said to him, "To you I will give their glory and all this authority; for it has been given over to me, and I give it to anyone I please. If you, then, will worship me, it will all be yours." Jesus answered him, "It is written, 'Worship the Lord your God, and serve only him.'" Then the devil took him to Jerusalem, and placed him on the pinnacle of the temple, saying to him, "If you are the Son of God, throw yourself down from here, for it is written, 'He will command his angels concerning you, to protect you,' and 'On their hands they will bear you up, so that you will not dash your foot against a stone.'" Jesus answered him, "It is said, 'Do not put the Lord your God to the test.'" When the devil had finished every test, he departed from him until an opportune time.

The Last Temptation of Christ (1988) was the landmark film by Martin Scorsese (b. 1942) based on the original novel by Nikos Kazantzakis (1883-1957). Quite controversial when it landed in theaters, the film follows an alternative look at the life and death of Jesus Christ. Most provocative is the event the title alludes to—which is set up by the temptations in the wilderness: in this narrative, Jesus imagines his life if he accepts the devil's offer and comes down from the cross before dying.

George Herbert (1593-1633) was a Welsh-born Anglican priest and poet. This theologian and metaphysical poet is one of the Anglican Divines, a saintly man who put a definitive mark on Anglicanism for all time. For Herbert the baptism of Jesus prefigures his death for "my deare Redeemers pierced side."

Excerpt from *H. Baptisme*

I.

As he that sees a dark and shadie grove,
>> Stays not, but looks beyond it on the skie;
>> So when I view my sinnes, mine eyes remove
More backward still, and to that water flie,

Which is above the heav'ns, whose spring and vent
>> Is in my deare Redeemers pierced side.
>> O blessed streams! either ye do prevent
And stop our sinnes from growing thick and wide,

Or else give tears to drown them, as they grow.
        In you Redemption measures all my time,
        And spreads the plaister equall to the crime.
You taught the Book of Life my name, that so
        What ever future sinnes should me miscall,
        Your first acquaintance might discredit all

II.
Since, Lord, to thee
        A narrow way and little gate
Is all the passage, on my infancie
        Thou didst lay hold, and antedate
           My faith in me.

        O let me still
        Write thee great God, and me a childe:
Let me be soft and supple to thy will,
        Small to my self, to others milde,
           Behither ill.

        Although by stealth
        My flesh get on, yet let her sister
My soul bid nothing, but preserve her wealth:
        The growth of flesh is but a blister;
           Childhood is health

Jesus is hungry. The Devil is tempting. Being true to oneself while being tempted is hard. Being Jewish in the Netherlands during Nazi occupation was also hard. Anne Frank (1929-1945), a teenager living with her family in a secret annex during that time, kept a journal until she and her family were exposed and deported to the Bergen-Belsen camp, where all except her father died. After the war, her journal was published as *The Diary of a Young Girl*. In this entry, Anne continues to believe in "ideals" and "hope" despite the evil around her. She addresses the diary to her friend Kitty.

Saturday, 15 July, 1944.

Dear Kitty,

We have had a book from the library with the challenging title of: *What Do You Think of the Modern Young Girl?* I want to talk about this subject today . . .

"For in its innermost depths youth is lonelier than old age." I read this saying in some book and I've always remembered it, and found it to be true. Is it true then that grownups have a more difficult time here than we do? No I know it isn't . . .

Anyone who claims that the older ones have a more difficult time here certainly doesn't realize to what extent our problems weigh down on us, problems for which we are probably much too young, but which thrust themselves upon us continually, until, after a long time, we think we've found a solution, but the solution doesn't seem able to resist the facts which reduce it to nothing again. That's the difficulty in these times: ideals, dreams, and cherished hopes rise within us, only to meet the horrible truth and be shattered.

It's really a wonder that I haven't dropped all my ideals, because they seem so absurd and impossible to carry out. Yet I keep them, because in spite of everything I still believe that people are really good at heart. I simply can't build up my hopes on a foundation consisting of confusion, misery, and death. I see the world gradually being turned into a wilderness, I hear the ever approaching thunder, which will destroy us too. I can feel the sufferings of millions and yet, if I look up into the heavens, I think that it will all come right, that this cruelty too will end, and that peace and tranquility will return again.

In the meantime, I must uphold my ideals, for perhaps the time will come when I shall be able to carry them out.

Yours,
Anne.

Norman Maclean's (1902-1990) story *A River Runs through It* tells about a Scottish-American Presbyterian family from the perspective of the older son. At the end of the narrator's life, he finds the Blackfoot River a place of both connection and separation. The river grounds him and reminds him of separation. It is both wild and domestic.

Now nearly all those I loved and did not understand when I am young are dead, but still I reach out to them.

Of course, now I am too old to be much of a fisherman, and now of course I usually fish the waters alone, although some friends think I shouldn't. Like many fly fishermen in western Montana where the summer days are almost Arctic in length, I often do not start fishing until the cool of the evening. Then in the Arctic half-light of the canyon, all existence fades to a being with my soul and memories and the sounds of the Big Blackfoot River and a four-count rhythm and the hope that a fish will rise.

Eventually, all things merge into one, and a river runs through it. The river was cut by the world's great flood and runs over rocks from the basement of time. On some of the rocks are timeless raindrops. Under the rocks are the words, and some of the words are theirs.

I am haunted by waters.

THE SECOND SUNDAY IN LENT

Year A

John 3:1-17

There was a Pharisee named Nicodemus, a leader of the Jews. He came to Jesus by night and said to him, "Rabbi, we know that you are a teacher who has come from God; for no one can do these signs that you do apart from the presence of God." Jesus answered him, "Very truly, I tell you, no one can see the kingdom of God without being born from above." Nicodemus said to him, "How can anyone be born after having grown old? Can one enter a second time into the mother's womb and be born?" Jesus answered, "Very truly, I tell you, no one can enter the kingdom of God without being born of water and Spirit. What is born of the flesh is flesh, and what is born of the Spirit is spirit. Do not be astonished that I said to you, 'You must be born from above.' The wind blows where it chooses, and you hear the sound of it, but you do not know where it comes from or where it goes. So it is with everyone who is born of the Spirit." Nicodemus said to him, "How can these things be?" Jesus answered him, "Are you a teacher of Israel, and yet you do not understand these things? Very truly, I tell you, we speak of what we know and testify to what we have seen; yet you do not receive our testimony. If I have told you about earthly things and you do not believe, how can you believe if I tell you about heavenly things? No one has ascended into heaven except the one who descended from heaven, the Son of Man. And just as Moses lifted up the serpent in the wilderness, so must the Son of Man be lifted up, that whoever believes in him may have eternal life. For God so loved the world that he gave his only Son, so that everyone who believes in him may not perish but may have eternal life. Indeed, God did not send the Son into the world to condemn the world, but in order that the world might be saved through him."

Year B

Mark 8:31-38

Jesus began to teach his disciples that the Son of Man must undergo great suffering, and be rejected by the elders, the chief priests, and the scribes, and be killed, and after three days rise again. He said all this quite openly. And Peter took him aside and began to rebuke him. But turning and looking at his disciples, he rebuked Peter and said, "Get behind me, Satan! For you are setting your mind not on divine things but on human things." He called the crowd with his disciples, and said to them, "If any want to become my followers, let them deny themselves and take up their cross and follow me. For those who want to save their life will lose it, and those who lose their life for my sake, and for the sake of the gospel, will save it. For what will it profit them to gain the whole world and forfeit their life? Indeed, what can they give in return for their life? Those who are ashamed of me and of my words in this adulterous and sinful generation, of them the Son of Man will also be ashamed when he comes in the glory of his Father with the holy angels."

Year C

Luke 13:31-35

Some Pharisees came and said to Jesus, "Get away from here, for Herod wants to kill you." He said to them, "Go and tell that fox for me, 'Listen, I am casting out demons and performing cures today and tomorrow, and on the third day I finish my work. Yet today, tomorrow, and the next day I must be on my way, because it is impossible for a prophet to be killed outside of Jerusalem.' Jerusalem, Jerusalem, the city that kills the prophets and stones those who are sent to it! How often have I desired to gather your children together as a hen gathers her brood under her wings, and you were not willing! See, your house is left to you. And I tell you, you will not see me until the time comes when you say, 'Blessed is the one who comes in the name of the Lord.'"

Nicodemus comes by night to seek the God who was visible in Christ. Friedrich Nietzsche (1844-1900) tells this powerful parable of the "madman" who seeks God and informs the crowd that modernity has killed God. In the same way as Jesus tells Nicodemus the change made possible by God is as dramatic as being born again, so Nietzsche tells the crowd that deciding not to believe in God is as dramatic as wiping away the entire horizon.

Have you not heard of that madman who lit a lantern in the bright morning hours, ran to the market place, and cried incessantly: "I seek God! I seek God!"—As many of those who did not believe in God were standing around just then, he provoked much laughter. Has he got lost? asked one. Did he lose his way like a child? asked another. Or is he hiding? Is he afraid of us? Has he gone on a voyage? emigrated?—Thus they yelled and laughed.

The madman jumped into their midst and pierced them with his eyes. "Whither is God?" he cried; "I will tell you. *We have killed him*—you and I. All of us are his murderers. But how did we do this? How could we drink up the sea? Who gave us the sponge to wipe away the entire horizon? What were we doing when we unchained this earth from its sun? Whither is it moving now? Whither are we moving? Away from all suns? Are we not plunging continually? Backward, sideward, forward, in all directions? Is there still any up or down? Are we not straying, as through an infinite nothing? Do we not feel the breath of empty space? Has it not become colder? Is not night continually closing in on us? Do we not need to light lanterns in the morning? Do we hear nothing as yet of the noise of the gravediggers who are burying God? Do we smell nothing as yet of the divine decomposition? Gods, too, decompose. God is dead. God remains dead. And we have killed him.

"How shall we comfort ourselves, the murderers of all murderers? What was holiest and mightiest of all that the world has yet owned has bled to death under our knives: who will wipe this blood off us? What water is there for us to clean ourselves? What festivals of atonement, what sacred games shall we have to invent? Is not the greatness of this deed too great for us? Must we ourselves not become gods simply to appear worthy of it? There has never been a greater deed; and whoever is born after us—for the sake of this deed he will belong to a higher history than all history hitherto."

Here the madman fell silent and looked again at his listeners; and they, too, were silent and stared at him in astonishment. At last he threw his lantern on the ground, and it broke into pieces and went out. "I have come too early," he said then; "my time is not yet. This tremendous event is still on its way, still wandering; it has not yet reached the ears of men. Lightning and thunder require time; the light of the stars requires time; deeds, though done, still require time to be seen and heard. This deed is still more distant from them than most distant stars—*and yet they have done it themselves.*

It has been related further that on the same day the madman forced his way into several churches and there struck up his *requiem aeternam deo.* Led out and called to account, he is said always to have replied nothing but: "What after all are these churches now if they are not the tombs and sepulchers of God?"

Satan is a significant presence in Mark. Charles Baudelaire (1821-1867) was a French poet. He is best known for his volume of poems called *The Flowers of Evil*. His preoccupation with sex and death were distinctive and unusual themes for the time. "The Litanies of Satan" comes from this volume. Satanists love this poem and appreciate the way Mary is replaced by Satan.

O you, the most knowing, and loveliest of Angels,
a god fate betrayed, deprived of praises,
O Satan, take pity on my long misery!
O, Prince of exile to whom wrong has been done,
who, vanquished, always recovers more strongly,
O Satan, take pity on my long misery!
You who know everything, king of the underworld,
the familiar healer of human distress,
O Satan, take pity on my long misery!
You who teach even lepers, accursed pariahs,
through love itself the taste for Paradise,
O Satan, take pity on my long misery!
O you who on Death, your ancient true lover,
engendered Hope — that lunatic charmer!
O Satan, take pity on my long misery!
You who grant the condemned that calm, proud look
that damns a whole people crowding the scaffold,

O Satan, take pity on my long misery!
You who know in what corners of envious countries
a jealous God hid those stones that are precious,
O Satan, take pity on my long misery!
You whose clear eye knows the deep caches
where, buried, the race of metals slumbers,
O Satan, take pity on my long misery!
You whose huge hands hide the precipice,
from the sleepwalker on the sky-scraper's cliff,
O Satan, take pity on my long misery!
You who make magically supple the bones
of the drunkard, out late, who's trampled by horses,
O Satan, take pity on my long misery!
You who taught us to mix saltpetre with sulphur
to console the frail human being who suffers,
O Satan, take pity on my long misery!
You who set your mark, o subtle accomplice,
on the forehead of Croesus, the vile and pitiless,
O Satan, take pity on my long misery!
You who set in the hearts and eyes of young girls
the cult of the wound, adoration of rags,
O Satan, take pity on my long misery!
The exile's staff, the light of invention,
confessor to those to be hanged, to conspirators,
O Satan, take pity on my long misery!
Father, adopting those whom God the Father
drove in dark anger from the earthly paradise,
O Satan, take pity on my long misery!

This poem "Motor City Tirade" by Detroiter Dawn McDuffie captures both the wideness of the humanity Christ came to save, and the injustice that still plagues our cities. Like the embrace communicated in John 3:17, for the poet, Detroit is a place for all. Like Jesus's condemnation of Jerusalem in the pericope from Luke 13, the poet calls out powerful people who oppress the poor while building casinos for their own profit.

> Send us your homeless, your crazy.
> The lady who wears a wedding veil
> every day with her fox stoles and twenty necklaces—
> better she lives in the city; she would be locked up
> after one day on the clean streets
> of Bloomfield Hills.
> Hookers belong in the city
> just like wastewater sent in from the country
> in exchange for clean water pumped back
> for comfortable lives.
> Whole rivers flow under the pavements,
> constrained by tiles, carrying no light
> but still making a path to the Great Lakes.
> And hidden children in ghetto schools
> Breathe burning garbage,
> Roach droppings and asbestos dust,
> And flunk when they miss
> Too many days.
> They don't visit the shiny casino
> that displaced the local pool.
> Now we must host the happy gambler.
> Nothing as perfect as those casino streets
> edged with pots of geraniums.

Oh, it can be so pleasant here and also
near the mayor's house where the four-foot
snowfall is promptly whisked away
while the rest of us pray the electricity
won't give out. Aging circuits
keep the lights flickering. I watch them
Up and down the street from my house,
wires popping and writhing
when the load just gets too heavy.

"Losing one's life to save it" is a classic Jesus paradox. Christians are invited not to become too attached to the world or one's own life. Virginia Woolf (1882-1941), the modernist writer, captures the precariousness of life in this stream of consciousness that makes up her first short story "The Mark on the Wall." The narrator notices a mark on the wall. She then goes through various possibilities—a hook for a picture, a leaf, a crack in the wood, before finally being informed it is a snail. The theme of human ignorance and loss comes to the fore in this extract.

But as for that mark, I'm not sure about it; I don't believe it was made by a nail after all; it's too big, too round, for that. I might get up, but if I got up and looked at it, ten to one I shouldn't be able to say for certain; because once a thing's done, no one ever knows how it happened. Oh! dear me, the mystery of life; The inaccuracy of thought! The ignorance of humanity! To show how very little control of our possessions we have—what an accidental affair this living is after all our civilization—let me just count over a few of the things lost in one lifetime, beginning, for that seems always the most mysterious of losses—what cat would gnaw, what rat would nibble—three pale blue canisters of book-binding tools? Then there were the bird cages, the iron hoops, the steel skates, the Queen Anne coal-scuttle, the bagatelle board, the hand organ—all gone, and jewels, too. Opals and emeralds, they lie about the roots of turnips. What a scraping paring affair it is to be sure! The wonder is that I've any clothes on my back, that I sit surrounded by solid furniture at this moment. Why, if one wants to compare life to anything, one must liken it to being blown through the Tube* at fifty miles an hour— landing at the other end without a single hairpin in one's hair! Shot out at the feet of God entirely naked! Tumbling head over heels in the asphodel meadows like brown paper parcels pitched down a shoot in the post office! With one's hair flying back like the tail of a race-horse. Yes, that seems to express the rapidity of life, the perpetual waste and repair; all so casual, all so haphazard . . .

* The London Underground.

THE THIRD SUNDAY
IN LENT

Year A

John 4:5-42

Jesus came to a Samaritan city called Sychar, near the plot of ground that Jacob had given to his son Joseph. Jacob's well was there, and Jesus, tired out by his journey, was sitting by the well. It was about noon. A Samaritan woman came to draw water, and Jesus said to her, "Give me a drink." (His disciples had gone to the city to buy food.) The Samaritan woman said to him, "How is it that you, a Jew, ask a drink of me, a woman of Samaria?" (Jews do not share things in common with Samaritans.) Jesus answered her, "If you knew the gift of God, and who it is that is saying to you, 'Give me a drink,' you would have asked him, and he would have given you living water." The woman said to him, "Sir, you have no bucket, and the well is deep. Where do you get that living water? Are you greater than our ancestor Jacob, who gave us the well, and with his sons and his flocks drank from it?" Jesus said to her, "Everyone who drinks of this water will be thirsty again, but those who drink of the water that I will give them will never be thirsty. The water that I will give will become in them a spring of water gushing up to eternal life." The woman said to him, "Sir, give me this water, so that I may never be thirsty or have to keep coming here to draw water." Jesus said to her, "Go, call your husband, and come back." The woman answered him, "I have no husband." Jesus said to her, "You are right in saying, 'I have no husband'; for you have had five husbands, and the one you have now is not your husband. What you have said is true!" The woman said to him, "Sir, I see that you are a prophet. Our ancestors worshiped on this mountain, but you say that the place where people must worship is in Jerusalem." Jesus said to her, "Woman, believe me, the hour is coming when you will worship the Father neither on this mountain nor in Jerusalem. You worship what you do not know; we worship what we know, for salvation is from the Jews. But the hour is coming, and is now here, when the true worshipers will worship the Father in spirit and truth, for the Father seeks such as these to worship him. God is spirit, and those who worship him must worship in spirit and truth." The woman said to him, "I know that Messiah is coming" (who is called Christ). "When he comes, he will proclaim all things to us." Jesus said to her, "I am he, the one who is speaking to you." Just then his disciples came. They were astonished that he was speaking with a woman, but no one said, "What do you want?" or, "Why are you speaking with her?" Then the woman left her water jar and went back to the city. She said to the people, "Come and see a man who told me everything I have ever done! He cannot be the Messiah, can he?" They left the city and were on their way to him. Meanwhile the disciples were urging him, "Rabbi, eat something." But he said to them, "I have food to eat that you do not know about." So the disciples said to one another, "Surely no one has brought him something to eat?" Jesus said to them, "My food is to do the will of him who sent me and to complete his work. Do you not say, 'Four months more, then comes the harvest'? But I tell you, look around you, and see how the fields are ripe for harvesting. The reaper is already receiving wages and is gathering fruit for eternal life, so that sower and reaper may rejoice together. For here the saying holds true, 'One sows and another reaps.' I sent you to reap that for which you did not labor. Others have labored, and you have entered into their labor." Many Samaritans from that city believed in him because of the woman's testimony, "He told me everything I have ever done." So when the Samaritans came to him, they asked him to stay with them; and he stayed there two days. And many more believed because of his word. They said to the woman, "It is no longer because of what you said that we believe, for we have heard for ourselves, and we know that this is truly the Savior of the world."

Year B

John 2:13-22

The Passover of the Jews was near, and Jesus went up to Jerusalem. In the temple he found people selling cattle, sheep, and doves, and the money changers seated at their tables. Making a whip of cords, he drove all of them out of the temple, both the sheep and the cattle. He also poured out the coins of the money changers and overturned their tables. He told those who were selling the doves, "Take these things out of here! Stop making my Father's house a marketplace!" His disciples remembered that it was written, "Zeal for your house will consume me." The Jews then said to him, "What sign can you show us for doing this?" Jesus answered them, "Destroy this temple, and in three days I will raise it up." The Jews then said, "This temple has been under construction for forty-six years, and will you raise it up in three days?" But he was speaking of the temple of his body. After he was raised from the dead, his disciples remembered that he had said this; and they believed the scripture and the word that Jesus had spoken.

Year C

Luke 13:1-9

At that very time there were some present who told Jesus about the Galileans whose blood Pilate had mingled with their sacrifices. He asked them, "Do you think that because these Galileans suffered in this way they were worse sinners than all other Galileans? No, I tell you; but unless you repent, you will all perish as they did. Or those eighteen who were killed when the tower of Siloam fell on them—do you think that they were worse offenders than all the others living in Jerusalem? No, I tell you; but unless you repent, you will all perish just as they did." Then he told this parable: "A man had a fig tree planted in his vineyard; and he came looking for fruit on it and found none. So he said to the gardener, 'See here! For three years I have come looking for fruit on this fig tree, and still I find none. Cut it down! Why should it be wasting the soil?' He replied, 'Sir, let it alone for one more year, until I dig around it and put manure on it. If it bears fruit next year, well and good; but if not, you can cut it down.'"

The Samaritan woman of John 4 seeks to know the truth: she wants the eternal water of life. This yearning for the eternal truth is beautifully captured in the short story called "The Library of Babel" by Jorge Luis Borges (1899-1986). He was from Argentina, best known for his short stories, and a major figure in Spanish-language literature. This story is about a library which has every conceivable book that letters and punctuation could produce. The majority of books will be gibberish, but also the library would contain the truth about your future as well as every conceivable falsehood about your life. Unlike the encounter with Jesus, the library is an endless quest for a truth at which you never arrive.

> The universe (which others call the Library) is composed of an indefinite and perhaps infinite number of hexagonal galleries, with vast air shafts between, surrounded by very low railings. From any of the hexagons one can see, interminably, the upper and lower floors. The distribution of the galleries is invariable. Twenty shelves, five long shelves per side, cover all the sides except two; their height, which is the distance from floor to ceiling, scarcely exceeds that of a normal bookcase. One of the free sides leads to a narrow hallway which opens onto another gallery, identical to the first and to all the rest. To the left and right of the hallway there are two very small closets. In the first, one may sleep standing up; in the other, satisfy one's fecal necessities. Also through here passes a spiral stairway, which sinks abysmally and soars upwards to remote distances. In the hallway there is a mirror which faithfully duplicates all appearances. Men usually infer from this mirror

that the Library is not infinite (if it were, why this illusory duplication?); I prefer to dream that its polished surfaces represent and promise the infinite . . . Light is provided by some spherical fruit which bear the name of lamps. There are two, transversally placed, in each hexagon. The light they emit is insufficient, incessant.

Like all men of the Library, I have traveled in my youth; I have wandered in search of a book, perhaps the catalogue of catalogues; now that my eyes can hardly decipher what I write, I am preparing to die just a few leagues from the hexagon in which I was born. Once I am dead, there will be no lack of pious hands to throw me over the railing; my grave will be the fathomless air; my body will sink endlessly and decay and dissolve in the wind generated by the fall, which is infinite. I say that the Library is unending . . .

This thinker observed that all the books, no matter how diverse they might be, are made up of the same elements: the space, the period, the comma, the twenty-two letters of the alphabet. He also alleged a fact which travelers have confirmed: *In the vast Library there are no two identical books.* From these two incontrovertible premises he deduced that the Library is total and that its shelves register all the possible combinations of the twenty-odd orthographical symbols (a number which, though extremely vast, is not infinite): Everything: the minutely detailed history of the future, the archangels' autobiographies, the faithful catalogues of the Library, thousands and thousands of false catalogues, the demonstration of the fallacy of those catalogues, the demonstration of the fallacy of the true catalogue, the Gnostic gospel of Basilides, the commentary on that gospel, the commentary on the commentary on that gospel, the true story of your death, the translation of every book in all languages, the interpolations of every book in all books . . .

When it was proclaimed that the Library contained all books, the first impression was one of extravagant happiness. All men felt themselves to be the masters of an intact and secret treasure. There was no personal or world problem whose eloquent solution did not exist in some hexagon. The universe was justified, the universe suddenly usurped the unlimited dimensions of hope. At that time a great deal was said about the Vindications: books of apology and prophecy which vindicated for all time the acts of every man in the universe and retained prodigious arcana for his future. Thousands of the greedy abandoned their sweet native hexagons and rushed up the stairways, urged on by the vain intention of finding their Vindication. These pilgrims disputed in the narrow corridors, proffered dark curses, strangled each other on the divine stairways, flung the deceptive books into the air shafts, met their death cast down in a similar fashion by the inhabitants of remote regions. Others went mad . . . The Vindications exist (I have seen two which refer to persons of the future, to persons who are perhaps not imaginary) but the searchers did not remember that the possibility of a man's finding his Vindication, or some treacherous variation thereof, can be computed as zero.

At that time it was also hoped that a clarification of humanity's basic mysteries—the origin of the Library and of time—might be found. It is verisimilar that these grave mysteries could be explained in words: if the language of philosophers is not sufficient, the multiform Library will have produced the unprecedented language required, with its vocabularies and grammars. For four centuries now men have exhausted the hexagons . . . There are official searchers, *inquisitors*. I have seen them in the performance of their function: they always arrive extremely tired from their journeys; they speak of a broken stairway which almost killed them; they talk with the librarian of galleries and stairs; sometimes they pick up the nearest volume and leaf through it, looking for infamous words. Obviously, no one expects to discover anything.

As was natural, this inordinate hope was followed by an excessive depression. The certitude that some shelf in some hexagon held precious books and that these precious books were inaccessible, seemed almost intolerable.

Walter Brueggemann's (b. 1933) poem, "Marked by Ashes," helps us reorient our lives to God. There is no better time than Lent to readjust or to reset our lives through prayer and self-denial. Lent is the season that begins by marking us with ashes but then moves us with a steady cadence to a more perfect relationship with God.

> Ruler of the Night, Guarantor of the day . . .
> This day—a gift from you.
> This day—like none other you have ever given, or we have
> ever received.
> This Wednesday dazzles us with gift and newness and
> possibility.
> *This Wednesday burdens us with the tasks of the day, for we*
> *are already*
> > *halfway home*
> > *halfway back to committees and memos,*
> > *halfway back to calls and appointments,*
> > *halfway on to next Sunday,*
> > *halfway back, half frazzled, half expectant,*
> > *half turned toward you, half rather not.*
> *This Wednesday is a long way from Ash Wednesday,*
> > *but all our Wednesdays are marked by ashes —*
> > *we begin this day with that et al.*

In Luke, Jesus explains that we need to make good use of every moment. Like the fig tree, we need to bear fruit. Rudyard Kipling (1865-1936) wrote this powerful poem, "If," inviting us to fill every minute with every distance run.

If you can keep your head when all about you
    Are losing theirs and blaming it on you,
If you can trust yourself when all men doubt you,
    But make allowance for their doubting too;
If you can wait and not be tired by waiting,
    Or being lied about, don't deal in lies,
Or being hated, don't give way to hating,
    And yet don't look too good, nor talk too wise:

If you can dream—and not make dreams your master;
    If you can think—and not make thoughts your aim;
If you can meet with Triumph and Disaster
    And treat those two impostors just the same;
If you can bear to hear the truth you've spoken
    Twisted by knaves to make a trap for fools,
Or watch the things you gave your life to, broken,
    And stoop and build 'em up with worn-out tools:

If you can make one heap of all your winnings
    And risk it on one turn of pitch-and-toss,
And lose, and start again at your beginnings
    And never breathe a word about your loss;
If you can force your heart and nerve and sinew
    To serve your turn long after they are gone,
And so hold on when there is nothing in you
    Except the Will which says to them: 'Hold on!'

If you can talk with crowds and keep your virtue,
    Or walk with Kings—nor lose the common touch,
If neither foes nor loving friends can hurt you,
    If all men count with you, but none too much;
If you can fill the unforgiving minute
    With sixty seconds' worth of distance run,
Yours is the Earth and everything that's in it,
    And—which is more—you'll be a Man, my son!

Luke's Gospel this day highlights the human capacity to perceive others as less—or at least, those with problems. This prompts Jesus to use his fig tree parable about owning up to these shortcomings. This theme is captured with great power in the Pulitzer Prize-winning play *A Delicate Balance* by Edward Albee (1928-2016). The play explores the possibility that humans may be too timid to confront these incapacities, as in Luke's narrative. Near the conclusion of the play, the character Edna muses to another main character, Agnes, about the challenge of realizing that the problem is, in fact, oneself.

THE FOURTH SUNDAY
IN LENT

Year A

John 9:1-41

As Jesus walked along, he saw a man blind from birth. His disciples asked him, "Rabbi, who sinned, this man or his parents, that he was born blind?" Jesus answered, "Neither this man nor his parents sinned; he was born blind so that God's works might be revealed in him. We must work the works of him who sent me while it is day; night is coming when no one can work. As long as I am in the world, I am the light of the world." When he had said this, he spat on the ground and made mud with the saliva and spread the mud on the man's eyes, saying to him, "Go, wash in the pool of Siloam" (which means Sent). Then he went and washed and came back able to see. The neighbors and those who had seen him before as a beggar began to ask, "Is this not the man who used to sit and beg?" Some were saying, "It is he." Others were saying, "No, but it is someone like him." He kept saying, "I am the man." But they kept asking him, "Then how were your eyes opened?" He answered, "The man called Jesus made mud, spread it on my eyes, and said to me, 'Go to Siloam and wash.' Then I went and washed and received my sight." They said to him, "Where is he?" He said, "I do not know." They brought to the Pharisees the man who had formerly been blind. Now it was a Sabbath day when Jesus made the mud and opened his eyes. Then the Pharisees also began to ask him how he had received his sight. He said to them, "He put mud on my eyes. Then I washed, and now I see." Some of the Pharisees said, "This man is not from God, for he does not observe the Sabbath." But others said, "How can a man who is a sinner perform such signs?" And they were divided. So they said again to the blind man, "What do you say about him? It was your eyes he opened." He said, "He is a prophet." The Jews did not believe that he had been blind and had received his sight until they called the parents of the man who had received his sight and asked them, "Is this your son, who you say was born blind? How then does he now see?" His parents answered, "We know that this is our son, and that he was born blind; but we do not know how it is that now he sees, nor do we know who opened his eyes. Ask him; he is of age. He will speak for himself." His parents said this because they were afraid of the Jews; for the Jews had already agreed that anyone who confessed Jesus to be the Messiah would be put out of the synagogue. Therefore his parents said, "He is of age; ask him." So for the second time they called the man who had been blind, and they said to him, "Give glory to God! We know that this man is a sinner." He answered, "I do not know whether he is a sinner. One thing I do know, that though I was blind, now I see." They said to him, "What did he do to you? How did he open your eyes?" He answered them, "I have told you already, and you would not listen. Why do you want to hear it again? Do you also want to become his disciples?" Then they reviled him, saying, "You are his disciple, but we are disciples of Moses. We know that God has spoken to Moses, but as for this man, we do not know where he comes from." The man answered, "Here is an astonishing thing! You do not know where he comes from, and yet he opened my eyes. We know that God does not listen to sinners, but he does listen to one who worships him and obeys his will. Never since the world began has it been heard that anyone opened the eyes of a person born blind. If this man were not from God, he could do nothing." They answered him, "You were born entirely in sins, and are you trying to teach us?" And they drove him out. Jesus heard that they had driven him out, and when he found him, he said, "Do you believe in the Son of Man?" He answered, "And who is he, sir? Tell me, so that I may believe in him." Jesus said to him, "You have seen him, and the one speaking with you is he." He said, "Lord, I believe." And he worshiped him. Jesus said, "I came into this world for judgment so that those who do not see may see, and those who do see may become blind." Some of the Pharisees near him heard this and said to him, "Surely we are not blind, are we?" Jesus said to them, "If you were blind, you would not have sin. But now that you say, 'We see,' your sin remains."

John 3:14-21

Jesus said, "Just as Moses lifted up the serpent in the wilderness, so must the Son of Man be lifted up, that whoever believes in him may have eternal life. For God so loved the world that he gave his only Son, so that everyone who believes in him may not perish but may have eternal life. Indeed, God did not send the Son into the world to condemn the world, but in order that the world might be saved through him. Those who believe in him are not condemned; but those who do not believe are condemned already, because they have not believed in the name of the only Son of God. And this is the judgment, that the light has come into the world, and people loved darkness rather than light because their deeds were evil. For all who do evil hate the light and do not come to the light, so that their deeds may not be exposed. But those who do what is true come to the light, so that it may be clearly seen that their deeds have been done in God."

Luke 15:1-3, 11b-32

All the tax collectors and sinners were coming near to listen to Jesus. And the Pharisees and the scribes were grumbling and saying, "This fellow welcomes sinners and eats with them." So Jesus told them this parable: "There was a man who had two sons. The younger of them said to his father, 'Father, give me the share of the property that will belong to me.' So he divided his property between them. A few days later the younger son gathered all he had and traveled to a distant country, and there he squandered his property in dissolute living. When he had spent everything, a severe famine took place throughout that country, and he began to be in need. So he went and hired himself out to one of the citizens of that country, who sent him to his fields to feed the pigs. He would gladly have filled himself with the pods that the pigs were eating; and no one gave him anything. But when he came to himself he said, 'How many of my father's hired hands have bread enough and to spare, but here I am dying of hunger! I will get up and go to my father, and I will say to him, "Father, I have sinned against heaven and before you; I am no longer worthy to be called your son; treat me like one of your hired hands."' So he set off and went to his father. But while he was still far off, his father saw him and was filled with compassion; he ran and put his arms around him and kissed him. Then the son said to him, 'Father, I have sinned against heaven and before you; I am no longer worthy to be called your son.' But the father said to his slaves, 'Quickly, bring out a robe—the best one—and put it on him; put a ring on his finger and sandals on his feet. And get the fatted calf and kill it, and let us eat and celebrate; for this son of mine was dead and is alive again; he was lost and is found!' And they began to celebrate. Now his elder son was in the field; and when he came and approached the house, he heard music and dancing. He called one of the slaves and asked what was going on. He replied, 'Your brother has come, and your father has killed the fatted calf, because he has got him back safe and sound.' Then he became angry and refused to go in. His father came out and began to plead with him. But he answered his father, 'Listen! For all these years I have been working like a slave for you, and I have never disobeyed your command; yet you have never given me even a young goat so that I might celebrate with my friends. But when this son of yours came back, who has devoured your property with prostitutes, you killed the fatted calf for him!' Then the father said to him, 'Son, you are always with me, and all that is mine is yours. But we had to celebrate and rejoice, because this brother of yours was dead and has come to life; he was lost and has been found.'"

The lectionary reading from John 9 starts with one of the oldest and hardest faith questions: Who is to blame for a person blind from birth? The temptation is to blame "original sin." Lawrence Raab (b. 1946) is an American poet, who has been a professor at several major universities. In this poem, "Original Sin," he muses on the need for faith to be rational.

That was one idea my mother
always disliked. She preferred her god
to be reasonable, like Emerson or Thoreau
without their stranger moments.
Even the Old Testament God's
sudden angers and twisted ways
of getting what he wanted she'd accept
as metaphor. But original sin
was different. Plus no one agreed
if it was personal, meaning
all Adam's fault, or else some kind
of temporary absence of the holy,
which was Adam's fault as well.
In any case, it made no sense
that we'd need to be saved before
we'd even had the chance to be wrong.
Yes, eventually everyone
falls into error, but when my sister and I
were babies she could see we were perfect,
as we opened our eyes and gazed up at her
with what she took for granted as love,
long before either of us knew the word
and what damage it could cause.

Henry Wadsworth Longfellow (1807-1882) was an American educator and poet. In *Part I, The Divine Tragedy (The Second Passover, IV. Nicodemus at Night)*, Longfellow asserts that the Son of Man must be lifted up, yes crucified, so that none will perish and that all may have life eternal.

CHRISTUS.
And as Moses
Uplifted the serpent in the wilderness,
So must the Son of Man be lifted up;
That whosoever shall believe in Him
Shall perish not, but have eternal life.
He that believes in Him is not condemned;
He that believes not, is condemned already.

NICODEMUS, *aside.*
He speaketh like a Prophet of the Lord!

CHRISTUS.
This is the condemnation; that the light
Is come into the world, and men loved darkness
Rather than light, because their deeds are evil!

NICODEMUS, *aside.*
Of me he speaketh! He reproveth me,
Because I come by night to question him!

CHRISTUS.
For every one that doeth evil deeds
Hateth the light, nor cometh to the light,
Lest he should be reproved.

NICODEMUS, *aside.*

Alas, how truly
He readeth what is passing in my heart!

CHRISTUS.

But he that doeth truth comes to the light
So that his deeds may be made manifest,
That they are wrought in God.

NICODEMUS.

Alas! alas!

Henri Nouwen (1932-1996) was a Dutch Catholic priest, professor, theologian and writer. Increasingly, he became concerned about social justice and community. In his later years he always traveled with a companion who was developmentally challenged. His book, *The Return of the Prodigal Son: A Story of Homecoming,* was inspired by his encounter with a reproduction of Rembrandt's *Prodigal Son.* The short story is a moment in Nouwen's long, spiritual adventure. Like the Prodigal Son in Luke's Gospel, Nouwen's life was a journey home to God.

> For most of my life I have struggled to find God, to know God, to love God. I have tried hard to follow the guidelines of the spiritual life—pray always, work for others, read the Scriptures—and to avoid the many temptations to dissipate myself. I have failed many times but always tried again, even when I was close to despair.
>
> Now I wonder whether I have sufficiently realized that during all this time God has been trying to find me, to know me, and to love me. The question is not "How am I to find God?" but "How am I to let myself be found by him?" The question is not "How am I to know God?" but "How am I to let myself be known by God?" And, finally, the questions is not "How am I to love God?" but How am I to let myself be loved by God?" God is looking into the distance for me, trying to find me, and longing to bring me home.

In John's famous passage, John 3:16, Nicodemus learns of Jesus's purpose—sent by God for the purpose of salvation. Jerry Siegel and Joe Shuster's iconic comic book character Superman has a backstory that relies heavily on Judeo-Christian themes. But the 1978 cinematic adaptation of *Superman* directed by Richard Donner (b. 1930) emphasized that theology even further. A young child is sent by rocket ship to Earth, where he obtains superpowers and grows into the persona of "Superman," performing heroic acts while keeping a secret identity as mild-mannered reporter Clark Kent. In this majestic film, which started the modern comic-book-movie craze some 40 years ago, a young Clark Kent realizes he is quite special and constructs his Fortress of Solitude in the North Pole. There, he communes with the spirit of his father, Jor-El, who tells him in not-so-subtle terms that he is to be the savior of the human race—even using language comparing him to a Christ-like light in the world.

THE FIFTH SUNDAY
IN LENT

Year A

John 11:1-45

Now a certain man was ill, Lazarus of Bethany, the village of Mary and her sister Martha. Mary was the one who anointed the Lord with perfume and wiped his feet with her hair; her brother Lazarus was ill. So the sisters sent a message to Jesus, "Lord, he whom you love is ill." But when Jesus heard it, he said, "This illness does not lead to death; rather it is for God's glory, so that the Son of God may be glorified through it." Accordingly, though Jesus loved Martha and her sister and Lazarus, after having heard that Lazarus was ill, he stayed two days longer in the place where he was.

Then after this he said to the disciples, "Let us go to Judea again." The disciples said to him, "Rabbi, the Jews were just now trying to stone you, and are you going there again?" Jesus answered, "Are there not twelve hours of daylight? Those who walk during the day do not stumble, because they see the light of this world. But those who walk at night stumble, because the light is not in them." After saying this, he told them, "Our friend Lazarus has fallen asleep, but I am going there to awaken him." The disciples said to him, "Lord, if he has fallen asleep, he will be all right." Jesus, however, had been speaking about his death, but they thought that he was referring merely to sleep. Then Jesus told them plainly, "Lazarus is dead. For your sake I am glad I was not there, so that you may believe. But let us go to him." Thomas, who was called the Twin, said to his fellow disciples, "Let us also go, that we may die with him." When Jesus arrived, he found that Lazarus had already been in the tomb four days. Now Bethany was near Jerusalem, some two miles away, and many of the Jews had come to Martha and Mary to console them about their brother. When Martha heard that Jesus was coming, she went and met him, while Mary stayed at home. Martha said to Jesus, "Lord, if you had been here, my brother would not have died. But even now I know that God will give you whatever you ask of him." Jesus said to her, "Your brother will rise again." Martha said to him, "I know that he will rise again in the resurrection on the last day." Jesus said to her, "I am the resurrection and the life. Those who believe in me, even though they die, will live, and everyone who lives and believes in me will never die. Do you believe this?" She said to him, "Yes, Lord, I believe that you are the Messiah, the Son of God, the one coming into the world."

When she had said this, she went back and called her sister Mary, and told her privately, "The Teacher is here and is calling for you." And when she heard it, she got up quickly and went to him. Now Jesus had not yet come to the village, but was still at the place where Martha had met him. The Jews who were with her in the house, consoling her, saw Mary get up quickly and go out. They followed her because they thought that she was going to the tomb to weep there. When Mary came where Jesus was and saw him, she knelt at his feet and said to him, "Lord, if you had been here, my brother would not have died." When Jesus saw her weeping, and the Jews who came with her also weeping, he was greatly disturbed in spirit and deeply moved. He said, "Where have you laid him?" They said to him, "Lord, come and see." Jesus began to weep. So the Jews said, "See how he loved him!" But some of them said, "Could not he who opened the eyes of the blind man have kept this man from dying?" Then Jesus, again greatly disturbed, came to the tomb. It was a cave, and a stone was lying against it. Jesus said, "Take away the stone." Martha, the sister of the dead man, said to him, "Lord, already there is a stench because he has been dead four days." Jesus said to her, "Did I not tell you that if you believed, you would see the glory of God?" So they took away the stone. And Jesus looked upward and said, "Father, I thank you for having heard me. I knew that you always hear me, but I have said this for the sake of the crowd standing here, so that they may believe that you sent me." When he had said this, he cried with a loud voice, "Lazarus, come out!" The dead man came out, his hands and feet bound with strips of cloth, and his face wrapped in a cloth. Jesus said to them, "Unbind him, and let him go." Many of the Jews therefore, who had come with Mary and had seen what Jesus did, believed in him.

John 12:20-33

Now among those who went up to worship at the festival were some Greeks. They came to Philip, who was from Bethsaida in Galilee, and said to him, "Sir, we wish to see Jesus." Philip went and told Andrew; then Andrew and Philip went and told Jesus. Jesus answered them, "The hour has come for the Son of Man to be glorified. Very truly, I tell you, unless a grain of wheat falls into the earth and dies, it remains just a single grain; but if it dies, it bears much fruit. Those who love their life lose it, and those who hate their life in this world will keep it for eternal life. Whoever serves me must follow me, and where I am, there will my servant be also. Whoever serves me, the Father will honor. Now my soul is troubled. And what should I say— 'Father, save me from this hour'? No, it is for this reason that I have come to this hour. Father, glorify your name." Then a voice came from heaven, "I have glorified it, and I will glorify it again." The crowd standing there heard it and said that it was thunder. Others said, "An angel has spoken to him." Jesus answered, "This voice has come for your sake, not for mine. Now is the judgment of this world; now the ruler of this world will be driven out. And I, when I am lifted up from the earth, will draw all people to myself." He said this to indicate the kind of death he was to die.

Year C

John 12:1-8

Six days before the Passover Jesus came to Bethany, the home of Lazarus, whom he had raised from the dead. There they gave a dinner for him. Martha served, and Lazarus was one of those at the table with him. Mary took a pound of costly perfume made of pure nard, anointed Jesus' feet, and wiped them with her hair. The house was filled with the fragrance of the perfume. But Judas Iscariot, one of his disciples (the one who was about to betray him), said, "Why was this perfume not sold for three hundred denarii and the money given to the poor?" (He said this not because he cared about the poor, but because he was a thief; he kept the common purse and used to steal what was put into it.) Jesus said, "Leave her alone. She bought it so that she might keep it for the day of my burial. You always have the poor with you, but you do not always have me."

In the raising of Lazarus story, there is a central theme. What sort of God do we believe in? "God" by César Vallejo (1892-1938) captures the God revealed in Christ. César Abraham Vallejo Mendoza was a Peruvian poet and is considered one of the world's greatest poets of the twentieth century.

I feel that God is traveling
so much in me, with the dusk and the sea.
With him we go along together. It is getting dark.
With him we get dark. All orphans . . .

But I feel God. And it seems
that he sets aside some good color for me.
He is kind and sad, like those who care for the sick;
he whispers with sweet contempt like a lover's:
his heart must give him great pain.

Oh my God, I've only just come to you,
today I love so much in this twilight; today
that in the false balance of some breasts
I weigh and weep for a frail Creation.

And you, what do you weep for . . . you, in love
with such an immense and whirling breast . . .
I consecrate you, God, because you love so much;
because you never smile; because your heart
must all the time give you great pain.

Translation by Robert Bly.

———⚭———

The anticipation of death is a major theme in John's Gospel. It was D. H. Lawrence (1885-1930) who wrote movingly about death in his short story "Odour of Chrysanthemums." Elizabeth Bates is frustrated that her husband, Walter, is late for dinner. She suspects he is at the pub getting drunk. It transpires that he had died in the coal mine. All the ambivalent feelings about her marriage emerge in this excerpt as she washes his dead body with her mother-in-law.

When Elizabeth came down she found her mother alone on the parlour floor, leaning over the dead man, the tears dropping on him.

"We must lay him out," the wife said. She put on the kettle, then returning knelt at the feet, and began to unfasten the knotted leather laces. The room was clammy and dim with only one candle, so that she had to bend her face almost to the floor. At last she got off the heavy boots and put them away.

"You must help me now," she whispered to the old woman. Together they stripped the man.

When they arose, saw him lying in the naïve dignity of death, the women stood arrested in fear and respect. For a few moments they remained still, looking down, the old mother whimpering. Elizabeth felt countermanded. She saw him, how utterly inviolable he lay in himself. She had nothing to do with him. She could not accept it. Stooping, she laid her hand on him, in claim. He was still warm, for the mine was hot where he had died. His mother had his face between her hands, and was murmuring incoherently. The old tears fell in succession as drops from wet leaves; the mother was not weeping, merely her tears flowed. Elizabeth embraced the body of her husband, with cheek and lips. She seemed to be listening, inquiring, trying to get some connection. But she could not. She was driven away. He was impregnable.

She rose, went into the kitchen, where she poured warm water into a bowl, brought soap and flannel and a soft towel.

"I must wash him," she said.

Then the old mother rose stiffly, and watched Elizabeth as she carefully washed his face, carefully brushing the big blond moustache from his mouth with the flannel. She was afraid with a bottomless fear, so she ministered to him. The old woman, jealous, said: "Let me wipe him!"—and she kneeled on the other side drying slowly as Elizabeth washed, her big black bonnet sometimes brushing the dark head of her daughter. They worked thus in silence for a long time. They never forgot it was death, and the touch of the man's dead body gave them strange emotions, different in each of the women; a great dread possessed them both, the mother felt the lie was given to her womb, she was denied; the wife felt the utter isolation of the human soul, the child within her was a weight apart from her.

At last it was finished. He was a man of handsome body, and his face showed no traces of drink. He was blonde, full-fleshed, with fine limbs. But he was dead.

"Bless him," whispered his mother, looking always at his face, and speaking out of sheer terror. "Dear lad— bless him!" She spoke in a faint, sibilant ecstasy of fear and mother love.

Elizabeth sank down again to the floor, and put her face against his neck, and trembled and shuddered. But she had to draw away again. He was dead, and her living flesh had no place against his. A great dread and weariness held her: she was so unavailing. Her life was gone like this.

"White as milk he is, clear as a twelve-month baby, bless him, the darling!" the old mother murmured to herself. "Not a mark on him, clear and clean and white, beautiful as ever a child was made," she murmured with pride. Elizabeth kept her face hidden.

"He went peaceful, Lizzie—peaceful as sleep. Isn't he beautiful, the lamb? Ay—he must ha' made his peace, Lizzie. 'Appen he made it all right, Lizzie, shut in there. He'd have time. He wouldn't look like this if he hadn't made his peace. The lamb, the dear lamb. Eh, but he had a hearty laugh. I loved to hear it. He had the heartiest laugh, Lizzie, as a lad—"

Elizabeth looked up. The man's mouth was fallen back, slightly open under the cover of the moustache. The eyes, half shut, did not show glazed in the obscurity. Life with its smoky burning gone from him, had left him apart and utterly alien to her. And she knew what a stranger he was to her. In her womb was ice of fear, because of this separate stranger with whom she had been living as one flesh. Was this what it all meant—utter, intact separateness, obscured by heat of living? In dread she turned her face away. The fact was too deadly. There had been nothing between them, and yet they had come together, exchanging their nakedness repeatedly. Each time he had taken her, they had been two isolated beings, far apart as now. He was no more responsible than she. The child was like ice in her womb. For as she looked at the dead man, her mind, cold and detached, said clearly: "Who am I? What have I been doing? I have been fighting a husband who did not exist. HE existed all the time. What wrong have I done? What was that I have been living with? There lies the reality, this man."—And her soul died in her for fear: she knew she had never seen him, he had never seen her, they had met in the dark and had fought in the dark, not knowing whom they met nor whom they fought. And now she saw, and turned silent in seeing. For she had been wrong. She had said he was something he was not; she had felt familiar with him. Whereas he was apart all the while, living as she never lived, feeling as she never felt.

Judas plays an important role in John's Gospel generally and is a key character in the narrative concerning Mary and the costly perfume. Making sense of Judas is hard. This poem, sometimes attributed to Catholic priest Peter de Rosa (b. 1932) may be from unknown authorship. It draws parallels between Judas and Jesus, but the words are spoken by Jesus.

> Judas, if true love never ceases,
> how could you, my friend, have come to this:
> to sell me for thirty silver pieces,
> betray me with a kiss?
> Judas, remember what I taught you:
> do not despair while dangling on that rope.
> It's because you sinned that I sought you;
> I came to bring you hope.
>
> Judas, let's pray and hang together,
> you on your halter, I upon my hill.
> Dear friend even if you loved me never,
> you know I love you still.

There is a running theme of a "triumph of the human spirit" in Edward Zwick's (b. 1952) film, *Glory* (1989—the true story of the 54th Massachusetts Regiment in the American Civil War, which was comprised of African Americans, many of whom were ex-slaves; organized in 1863, it was the first such regiment to serve in the Union Army). The regiment is given the distinct honor of leading the assault on the Confederate Ft. Wagner in South Carolina, a task sure to produce many casualties. Vacillating between fear and the glory of performing this duty for a greater good, the soldiers of the 54th spend their last night prior to battle singing Christian hymns of deliverance and trust in God. As Mark's Gospel depicts Jesus addressing the temptation to ask God to "save him from this hour," so, too, does *Glory* depict that same complicated trust in God in the face of trial.

PALM SUNDAY

This is a complex Sunday. For gospel readings, we are reproducing only one illustration for the Liturgy of the Palms and the shorter versions of the Gospels for the Liturgy of the Word.

Liturgy of the Palms: Matthew 21:1-11

When Jesus and his disciples had come near Jerusalem and had reached Bethpage, at the Mount of Olives, Jesus sent two disciples, saying to them, "Go into the village ahead of you, and immediately you will find a donkey tied, and a colt with her; untie them and bring them to me. If anyone says anything to you, just say this, 'The Lord needs them.' And he will send them immediately." This took place to fulfill what had been spoken through the prophet, saying, "Tell the daughter of Zion, Look, your king is coming to you, humble, and mounted on a donkey, and on a colt, the foal of a donkey." The disciples went and did as Jesus had directed them; they brought the donkey and the colt, and put their cloaks on them, and he sat on them. A very large crowd spread their cloaks on the road, and others cut branches from the trees and spread them on the road. The crowds that went ahead of him and that followed were shouting, "Hosanna to the Son of David! Blessed is the one who comes in the name of the Lord! Hosanna in the highest heaven!" When he entered Jerusalem, the whole city was in turmoil, asking, "Who is this?" The crowds were saying, "This is the prophet Jesus from Nazareth in Galilee."

Liturgy of the Word

Year A

Matthew 27:11-54

Jesus stood before the governor; and the governor asked him, "Are you the King of the Jews?" Jesus said, "You say so." But when he was accused by the chief priests and elders, he did not answer. Then Pilate said to him, "Do you not hear how many accusations they make against you?" But he gave him no answer, not even to a single charge, so that the governor was greatly amazed. Now at the festival the governor was accustomed to release a prisoner for the crowd, anyone whom they wanted. At that time they had a notorious prisoner, called Jesus Barabbas. So after they had gathered, Pilate said to them, "Whom do you want me to release for you, Jesus Barabbas or Jesus who is called the Messiah?" For he realized that it was out of jealousy that they had handed him over. While he was sitting on the judgment seat, his wife sent word to him, "Have nothing to do with that innocent man, for today I have suffered a great deal because of a dream about him." Now the chief priests and the elders persuaded the crowds to ask for Barabbas and to have Jesus killed. The governor again said to them, "Which of the two do you want me to release for you?" And they said, "Barabbas." Pilate said to them, "Then what should I do with Jesus who is called the Messiah?" All of them said, "Let him be crucified!" Then he asked, "Why, what evil has he done?" But they shouted all the more, "Let him be crucified!" So when Pilate saw that he could do nothing, but rather that a riot was beginning, he took some water and washed his hands before the crowd, saying, "I am innocent of this man's blood; see to it yourselves." Then the people as a whole answered, "His blood be on us and on our children!" So he released Barabbas for them; and after flogging Jesus, he handed him over to be crucified. Then the soldiers of the governor took Jesus into the governor's headquarters, and they gathered the whole cohort around him. They stripped him and put a scarlet robe on him, and after twisting some thorns into a crown, they put it on his head. They put a reed in his right hand and knelt before him and mocked him, saying, "Hail, King of the Jews!" They spat on him, and took the reed and struck him on the head. After mocking him, they stripped him of the robe and put his own clothes on him. Then they led him away to crucify him. As they went out, they came upon a man from Cyrene named Simon; they compelled this man to carry his cross. And when they came to a place called Golgotha (which means Place of a Skull), they offered him wine to drink, mixed with gall; but when he tasted it, he would not drink it. And when they had crucified him, they divided his clothes among themselves by casting lots; then they sat down there and kept watch over him. Over his head they put the charge against him, which read, "This is Jesus, the King of the Jews." Then two bandits were crucified with him, one on his right and one on his left. Those who passed by derided him, shaking their heads and saying, "You who would destroy the temple and build it in three days, save yourself! If you are the Son of God, come down from the cross." In the same way the chief priests also, along with the scribes and elders, were mocking him, saying, "He saved others; he cannot save himself. He is the King of Israel; let him come down from the cross now, and we will believe in him.

He trusts in God; let God deliver him now, if he wants to; for he said, 'I am God's Son.'" The bandits who were crucified with him also taunted him in the same way. From noon on, darkness came over the whole land until three in the afternoon. And about three o'clock Jesus cried with a loud voice, "Eli, Eli, lema sabachthani?" that is, "My God, my God, why have you forsaken me?" When some of the bystanders heard it, they said, "This man is calling for Elijah." At once one of them ran and got a sponge, filled it with sour wine, put it on a stick, and gave it to him to drink. But the others said, "Wait, let us see whether Elijah will come to save him." Then Jesus cried again with a loud voice and breathed his last. At that moment the curtain of the temple was torn in two, from top to bottom. The earth shook, and the rocks were split. The tombs also were opened, and many bodies of the saints who had fallen asleep were raised. After his resurrection they came out of the tombs and entered the holy city and appeared to many. Now when the centurion and those with him, who were keeping watch over Jesus, saw the earthquake and what took place, they were terrified and said, "Truly this man was God's Son!"

Mark 15:1-39

As soon as it was morning, the chief priests held a consultation with the elders and scribes and the whole council. They bound Jesus, led him away, and handed him over to Pilate. Pilate asked him, "Are you the King of the Jews?" He answered him, "You say so." Then the chief priests accused him of many things. Pilate asked him again, "Have you no answer? See how many charges they bring against you." But Jesus made no further reply, so that Pilate was amazed. Now at the festival he used to release a prisoner for them, anyone for whom they asked. Now a man called Barabbas was in prison with the rebels who had committed murder during the insurrection. So the crowd came and began to ask Pilate to do for them according to his custom. Then he answered them, "Do you want me to release for you the King of the Jews?" For he realized that it was out of jealousy that the chief priests had handed him over. But the chief priests stirred up the crowd to have him release Barabbas for them instead. Pilate spoke to them again, "Then what do you wish me to do with the man you call the King of the Jews?" They shouted back, "Crucify him!" Pilate asked them, "Why, what evil has he done?" But they shouted all the more, "Crucify him!" So Pilate, wishing to satisfy the crowd, released Barabbas for them; and after flogging Jesus, he handed him over to be crucified. Then the soldiers led him into the courtyard of the palace (that is, the governor's headquarters); and they called together the whole cohort. And they clothed him in a purple cloak; and after twisting some thorns into a crown, they put it on him. And they began saluting him, "Hail, King of the Jews!" They struck his head with a reed, spat upon him, and knelt down in homage to him. After mocking him, they stripped him of the purple cloak and put his own clothes on him. Then they led him out to crucify him. They compelled a passer-by, who was coming in from the country, to carry his cross; it was Simon of Cyrene, the father of Alexander and Rufus. Then they brought Jesus to the place called Golgotha (which means the place of a skull). And they offered him wine mixed with myrrh; but he did not take it. And they crucified him, and divided his clothes among them, casting lots to decide what each should take. It was nine o'clock in the morning when they crucified him. The inscription of the charge against him read, "The King of the Jews." And with him they crucified two bandits, one on his right and one on his left. Those who passed by derided him, shaking their heads and saying, "Aha! You who would destroy the temple and build it in three days, save yourself, and come down from the cross!" In the same way the chief priests, along with the scribes, were also mocking him among themselves and saying, "He saved others; he cannot save himself. Let the Messiah, the King of Israel, come down from the cross now, so that we may see and believe." Those who were crucified with him also taunted him. When it was noon, darkness came over the whole land until three in the afternoon. At three o'clock Jesus cried out with a loud voice, "Eloi, Eloi, lema sabachthani?" which means, "My God, my God, why have you forsaken me?" When some of the bystanders heard it, they said, "Listen, he is calling for Elijah." And someone ran, filled a sponge with sour wine, put it on a stick, and gave it to him to drink, saying, "Wait, let us see whether Elijah will come to take him down." Then Jesus gave a loud cry and breathed his last. And the curtain of the temple was torn in two, from top to bottom. Now when the centurion, who stood facing him, saw that in this way he breathed his last, he said, "Truly this man was God's Son!"

Year C

Luke 23:1-49

The assembly of the elders of the people rose as a body and brought Jesus before Pilate. They began to accuse him, saying, "We found this man perverting our nation, forbidding us to pay taxes to the emperor, and saying that he himself is the Messiah, a king." Then Pilate asked him, "Are you the king of the Jews?" He answered, "You say so." Then Pilate said to the chief priests and the crowds, "I find no basis for an accusation against this man." But they were insistent and said, "He stirs up the people by teaching throughout all Judea, from Galilee where he began even to this place." When Pilate heard this, he asked whether the man was a Galilean. And when he learned that he was under Herod's jurisdiction, he sent him off to Herod, who was himself in Jerusalem at that time. When Herod saw Jesus, he was very glad, for he had been wanting to see him for a long time, because he had heard about him and was hoping to see him perform some sign. He questioned him at some length, but Jesus gave him no answer. The chief priests and the scribes stood by, vehemently accusing him. Even Herod with his soldiers treated him with contempt and mocked him; then he put an elegant robe on him, and sent him back to Pilate. That same day Herod and Pilate became friends with each other; before this they had been enemies. Pilate then called together the chief priests, the leaders, and the people, and said to them, "You brought me this man as one who was perverting the people; and here I have examined him in your presence and have not found this man guilty of any of your charges against him. Neither has Herod, for he sent him back to us. Indeed, he has done nothing to deserve death. I will therefore have him flogged and release him." Then they all shouted out together, "Away with this fellow! Release Barabbas for us!" (This was a man who had been put in prison for an insurrection that had taken place in the city, and for murder.) Pilate, wanting to release Jesus, addressed them again; but they kept shouting, "Crucify, crucify him!" A third time he said to them, "Why, what evil has he done? I have found in him no ground for the sentence of death; I will therefore have him flogged and then release him." But they kept urgently demanding with loud shouts that he should be crucified; and their voices prevailed. So Pilate gave his verdict that their demand should be granted. He released the man they asked for, the one who had been put in prison for insurrection and murder, and he handed Jesus over as they wished. As they led him away, they seized a man, Simon of Cyrene, who was coming from the country, and they laid the cross on him, and made him carry it behind Jesus. A great number of the people followed him, and among them were women who were beating their breasts and wailing for him. But Jesus turned to them and said, "Daughters of Jerusalem, do not weep for me, but weep for yourselves and for your children. For the days are surely coming when they will say, 'Blessed are the barren, and the wombs that never bore, and the breasts that never nursed.' Then they will begin to say to the mountains, 'Fall on us'; and to the hills, 'Cover us.' For if they do this when the wood is green, what will happen when it is dry?" Two others also, who were criminals, were led away to be put to death with him. When they came to the place that is called The Skull, they crucified Jesus there with the criminals, one on his right and one on his left. Then Jesus said, "Father, forgive them; for they do not know what they are doing." And they cast lots to divide his clothing. And the people stood by, watching; but the leaders scoffed at him, saying, "He saved others; let him save himself if he is the Messiah of God, his chosen one!" The soldiers also mocked him, coming up and offering him sour wine, and saying, "If you are the King of the Jews, save yourself!" There was also an inscription over him, "This is the King of the Jews." One of the criminals who were hanged there kept deriding him and saying, "Are you not the Messiah? Save yourself and us!" But the other rebuked him, saying, "Do you not fear God, since you are under the same sentence of condemnation? And we indeed have been condemned justly, for we are getting what we deserve for our deeds, but this man has done nothing wrong." Then he said, "Jesus, remember me when you come into your kingdom." He replied, "Truly I tell you, today you will be with me in Paradise." It was now about noon, and darkness came over the whole land until three in the afternoon, while the sun's light failed; and the curtain of the temple was torn in two. Then Jesus, crying with a loud voice, said, "Father, into your hands I commend my spirit." Having said this, he breathed his last. When the centurion saw what had taken place, he praised God and said, "Certainly this man was innocent." And when all the crowds who had gathered there for this spectacle saw what had taken place, they returned home, beating their breasts. But all his acquaintances, including the women who had followed him from Galilee, stood at a distance, watching these things.

The selections that follow are all suitable for the occasion: none is linked with a particular gospel.

Eichmann in Jerusalem: A Report on the Banality of Evil by Hannah Arendt (1906-1975) was originally published in 1963. The political theorist Arendt was a Jew who wrote this controversial classic on the Eichmann trial. Eichmann was part of Hitler's murder machine against the Jewish people. For Arendt, the single greatest discovery during the trial is that the Nazis, even those involved in evil atrocities, were just regular people. They were not psychopaths. Evil acts can be done by the most normal of people. This extract comes from the last page of her book.

> For when I speak of the banality of evil, I do so only on the strictly factual level, pointing to a phenomenon which stared one in the face at the trial. Eichmann was not Iago and not Macbeth, and nothing would have been farther from his mind than to determine with Richard III "to prove a villain." Except for an extraordinary diligence in looking out for his personal advancement, he had no motives at all. And this diligence in itself was in no way criminal; he certainly would never have murdered his superior in order to inherit his post. He merely, to put the matter colloquially, never realized what he was doing. It was precisely this lack of imagination which enabled him to sit for months on end facing a German Jew who was conducting the police interrogation, pouring out his heart to the man and explaining again and again how it was that he reached only the rank of lieutenant colonel

in the S.S. and that it had not been his fault that he was not promoted. In principle he knew quite well what it was all about, and in his final statement to the court he spoke of the "revaluation of values prescribed by the [Nazi] government." He was not stupid. It was sheer thoughtlessness—something by no means identical with stupidity—that predisposed him to become one of the greatest criminals of that period. And if this is "banal" and even funny, if with the best will in the world one cannot extract any diabolical or demonic profundity from Eichmann, that is still far from calling it commonplace. It surely cannot be so common that a man facing death, and, moreover, standing beneath the gallows, should be able to think of nothing but what he has heard at funerals all his life, and that these "lofty words" should completely becloud the reality of his own death. That such remoteness from reality and such thoughtlessness can wreak more havoc than all the evil instincts taken together which, perhaps, are inherent in man—that was, in fact, the lesson one could learn in Jerusalem.

The hymn "How Great Thou Art" is based on a traditional Swedish melody and poem, written by Carl Gustav Boberg (1859-1940). This beloved hymn was popularized by the Billy Graham Evangelistic Association in the latter half of the twentieth century. On Palm Sunday the cosmic order is shaken; a new creation is dawning; God does not "spare" his son; and Christ shall come with a shout of acclamation in the streets of Jerusalem the Holy and in all of God's redeemed creation. These great themes are embraced by Boberg in his famous hymn of praise.

> O Lord my God, When I in awesome wonder,
> Consider all the worlds Thy Hands have made;
> I see the stars, I hear the rolling thunder,
> Thy power throughout the universe displayed.
>
>> Then sings my soul, My Saviour God, to Thee,
>> How great Thou art, How great Thou art.
>> Then sings my soul, My Saviour God, to Thee,
>> How great Thou art, How great Thou art!
>
> When through the woods, and forest glades I wander,
> And hear the birds sing sweetly in the trees.
> When I look down, from lofty mountain grandeur
> And see the brook, and feel the gentle breeze. (Refrain)
>
> And when I think, that God, His Son not sparing;
> Sent Him to die, I scarce can take it in;
> That on the Cross, my burden gladly bearing,
> He bled and died to take away my sin. (Refrain)

When Christ shall come, with shout of acclamation,
And take me home, what joy shall fill my heart.
Then I shall bow, in humble adoration,
And then proclaim: "My God, how great Thou art!"
(Refrain)

The scene of the "triumphal entry" into Jerusalem in the Gospels has fascinated and inspired artists for centuries. The Italian painter Giotto di Bondone (ca. 1267-1337) worked at a key time in the history of the world, restoring ancient practices in the wake of Byzantine imperialism. His fresco (pictured) adorns the Arena Chapel in Padua, Italy, illustrating the drama of the entry of Christ and his disciples (moving left to right), and the complicated scene in Jerusalem that awaits (on the right).

Despair is at the heart of Mark's narrative of the crucifixion. It has just one saying from the cross—the cry of despair from Psalm 22. Sylvia Plath (1932-1963) was an extraordinary poet and novelist. For most of her life, she was clinically depressed, and, tragically, eventually she took her own life. Here, in her journal, as she describes her years at Smith College, she captures the loneliness that even companionship cannot heal.

> At home I rested and played; here, where I work, the routine is momentarily suspended and I am lost. There is no living being on earth at this moment except myself. I could walk down the halls, and empty rooms would yawn mockingly at me from every side. God, but life is loneliness, despite all the opiates, despite the shrill tinsel gaiety of "parties" with no purpose, despite the false grinning faces we all wear. And when at last you find someone to whom you feel you can pour out your soul, you stop in shock at the words you utter—they are so rusty, so ugly, so meaningless and feeble from being kept in the small cramped dark inside you so long. Yes, there is joy, fulfillment and companionship—but the loneliness of the soul in its appalling self-consciousness is horrible and overpowering.

MAUNDY THURSDAY

Year A, B, and C

John 13:1-17, 31b-35

Now before the festival of the Passover, Jesus knew that his hour had come to depart from this world and go to the Father. Having loved his own who were in the world, he loved them to the end. The devil had already put it into the heart of Judas son of Simon Iscariot to betray him. And during supper Jesus, knowing that the Father had given all things into his hands, and that he had come from God and was going to God, got up from the table, took off his outer robe, and tied a towel around himself. Then he poured water into a basin and began to wash the disciples' feet and to wipe them with the towel that was tied around him. He came to Simon Peter, who said to him, "Lord, are you going to wash my feet?" Jesus answered, "You do not know now what I am doing, but later you will understand." Peter said to him, "You will never wash my feet." Jesus answered, "Unless I wash you, you have no share with me." Simon Peter said to him, "Lord, not my feet only but also my hands and my head!" Jesus said to him, "One who has bathed does not need to wash, except for the feet, but is entirely clean. And you are clean, though not all of you." For he knew who was to betray him; for this reason he said, "Not all of you are clean." After he had washed their feet, had put on his robe, and had returned to the table, he said to them, "Do you know what I have done to you? You call me Teacher and Lord—and you are right, for that is what I am. So if I, your Lord and Teacher, have washed your feet, you also ought to wash one another's feet. For I have set you an example, that you also should do as I have done to you. Very truly, I tell you, servants are not greater than their master, nor are messengers greater than the one who sent them. If you know these things, you are blessed if you do them. Now the Son of Man has been glorified, and God has been glorified in him. If God has been glorified in him, God will also glorify him in himself and will glorify him at once. Little children, I am with you only a little longer. You will look for me; and as I said to the Jews so now I say to you, 'Where I am going, you cannot come.' I give you a new commandment, that you love one another. Just as I have loved you, you also should love one another. By this everyone will know that you are my disciples, if you have love for one another."

Maundy Thursday finds the Christian community gathered around a basin before gathering around a table for a shared meal. In John's Gospel, Jesus gets up from the table and does the unthinkable. He kneels at the feet of his disciples with a basin and begins a "towel ministry" of servanthood. Ambrose of Milan (c. 340-397) tells the serving Jesus that he himself is soiled and stained because of his followers. His followers need no water to wash the master's feet. Their tears will suffice.

> Jesus, I wish you would let me wash your feet, since it was through walking about in me that you soiled them. I wish you would give me the task of wiping the stains from your feet, because it was my behavior that put them there. But where can I get the running water I need to wash your feet? If I have no water, at least I have tears.

At the heart of the Maundy Thursday liturgy is the concept of relationships. The relationship of Jesus with the disciples is at the heart of the gospel narrative. One beautiful meditation on the relationship between Jesus and his mother is the Pieta. The Pieta, as carved by Michelangelo, is the grieving Mother who holds with loving care the dying Jesus. Just as Mary cradled Jesus, so she is the "maid's arms" as Jesus went to "the kind of death he was to die." The dour Welsh poet, R.S. Thomas (1913-2000), reminds that the cross of Christ is "untenanted" for the Lord is risen indeed!

> Always the same hills
> Crowd the horizon
> Remote witnesses
> Of the still scene
>
> And in the foreground
> The tall Cross,
> Sombre, untenanted,
> Aches for the Body
> That is back in the cradle
> Of a maid's arms.

Many people are uncomfortable with the liturgy of Maundy Thursday when it includes the washing of feet. Often people are designated as sinners who will be washed ceremoniously. The symbolic cleansing is awkward and somewhat embarrassing. Yet, Maundy Thursday is a stripping down to the basics, even as the altar is stripped bare at the end of the service in preparation for Good Friday. An unknown Ghanaian poet, translated by Thomas Stevenson Colvin (1925-2000), captures the complex simplicity of the sacramental act of foot-washing in the hymn "Jesu, Jesu, Fill Us with Your Love."

> Jesu, Jesu,
> fill us with your love,
> show us how to serve
> the neighbors we have from you.
>
> Kneels at the feet of his friends,
> silently washes their feet,
> Master who acts as a slave to them.
>
> Neighbors are rich and poor,
> neighbors are black and white,
> neighbors are nearby and far away.
>
> These are the ones we should serve,
> these are the ones we should love.
> All are neighbors to us and you.
>
> Loving puts on our knees,
> serving as though we were slaves;
> this is the way we should live with you.

As in all the days of Holy Week leading to the Passion, the disciple who betrayed Christ, Judas Iscariot, lurks in the shadows and in the background. Yet perhaps in each disciple there was a Judas. Lady Gaga (b. 1986) identifies Judas as "Just a holy fool, oh baby he's so cruel." Yet, she is "in love with Judas." In the lyrics of her song, "Judas," Lady Gaga becomes Judas' Mary Magdalene. She captures the way in which we can find the liar and the cheat attractive. The bad boy has a certain charm. Her song poses certain challenging questions: Can we be so ambiguous about the one who betrayed our Lord? Or was Judas part of God's mystery in the drama of Jesus's earthly life? Can even Judas be forgiven?

GOOD FRIDAY

John 18:1—19:42

Jesus went out with his disciples across the Kidron valley to a place where there was a garden, which he and his disciples entered. Now Judas, who betrayed him, also knew the place, because Jesus often met there with his disciples. So Judas brought a detachment of soldiers together with police from the chief priests and the Pharisees, and they came there with lanterns and torches and weapons. Then Jesus, knowing all that was to happen to him, came forward and asked them, "Whom are you looking for?" They answered, "Jesus of Nazareth." Jesus replied, "I am he." Judas, who betrayed him, was standing with them. When Jesus said to them, "I am he," they stepped back and fell to the ground. Again he asked them, "Whom are you looking for?" And they said, "Jesus of Nazareth." Jesus answered, "I told you that I am he. So if you are looking for me, let these men go." This was to fulfill the word that he had spoken, "I did not lose a single one of those whom you gave me." Then Simon Peter, who had a sword, drew it, struck the high priest's slave, and cut off his right ear. The slave's name was Malchus. Jesus said to Peter, "Put your sword back into its sheath. Am I not to drink the cup that the Father has given me?"

So the soldiers, their officer, and the Jewish police arrested Jesus and bound him. First they took him to Annas, who was the father-in-law of Caiaphas, the high priest that year. Caiaphas was the one who had advised the Jews that it was better to have one person die for the people.

Simon Peter and another disciple followed Jesus. Since that disciple was known to the high priest, he went with Jesus into the courtyard of the high priest, but Peter was standing outside at the gate. So the other disciple, who was known to the high priest, went out, spoke to the woman who guarded the gate, and brought Peter in. The woman said to Peter, "You are not also one of this man's disciples, are you?" He said, "I am not." Now the slaves and the police had made a charcoal fire because it was cold, and they were standing around it and warming themselves. Peter also was standing with them and warming himself.

Then the high priest questioned Jesus about his disciples and about his teaching. Jesus answered, "I have spoken openly to the world; I have always taught in synagogues and in the temple, where all the Jews come together. I have said nothing in secret. Why do you ask me? Ask those who heard what I said to them; they know what I said." When he had said this, one of the police standing nearby struck Jesus on the face, saying, "Is that how you answer the high priest?" Jesus answered, "If I have spoken wrongly, testify to the wrong. But if I have spoken rightly, why do you strike me?" Then Annas sent him bound to Caiaphas the high priest.

Now Simon Peter was standing and warming himself. They asked him, "You are not also one of his disciples, are you?" He denied it and said, "I am not." One of the slaves of the high priest, a relative of the man whose ear Peter had cut off, asked, "Did I not see you in the garden with him?" Again Peter denied it, and at that moment the cock crowed.

Then they took Jesus from Caiaphas to Pilate's headquarters. It was early in the morning. They themselves did not enter the headquarters, so as to avoid ritual defilement and to be able to eat the Passover. So Pilate went out to them and said, "What accusation do you bring against this man?" They answered, "If this man were not a criminal, we would not have handed him over to you." Pilate said to them, "Take him yourselves and judge him according to your law." The Jews replied, "We are not permitted to put anyone to death." (This was to fulfill what Jesus had said when he indicated the kind of death he was to die.)

Then Pilate entered the headquarters again, summoned Jesus, and asked him, "Are you the King of the Jews?" Jesus answered, "Do you ask this on your own, or did others tell you about me?" Pilate replied, "I am not a Jew, am I? Your own nation and the chief priests have handed you over to me. What have you done?" Jesus answered, "My kingdom is not from this world. If my kingdom were from this world, my followers would be fighting to keep me from being handed over to the Jews. But as it is, my kingdom is not from here." Pilate asked him, "So you are a king?" Jesus answered, "You say that I am a king. For this I was born, and for this I came into the world, to testify to the truth. Everyone who belongs to the truth listens to my voice." Pilate asked him, "What is truth?"

After he had said this, he went out to the Jews again and told them, "I find no case against him. But you have a custom that I release someone for you at the Passover. Do you want me to release for you the King of the Jews?" They shouted in reply, "Not this man, but Barabbas!" Now Barabbas was a bandit.

Then Pilate took Jesus and had him flogged. And the soldiers wove a crown of thorns and put it on his head, and they dressed him in a purple robe. They kept coming up to him, saying, "Hail, King of the Jews!" and striking him on the face. Pilate went out again and said to them, "Look, I am bringing him out to you to let you know that I find no case against him." So Jesus came out, wearing the crown of thorns and the purple robe. Pilate said to them, "Here is the man!" When the chief priests and the police saw him, they shouted, "Crucify him! Crucify him!" Pilate said to them, "Take him yourselves and crucify him; I find no case against him." The Jews answered him, "We have a law, and according to that law he ought to die because he has claimed to be the Son of God."

Now when Pilate heard this, he was more afraid than ever. He entered his headquarters again and asked Jesus, "Where are you from?" But Jesus gave him no answer. Pilate therefore said to him, "Do you refuse to speak to me? Do you not know that I have power to release you, and power to crucify you?" Jesus answered him, "You would have no power over me unless it had been given you from above; therefore the one who handed me over to you is guilty of a greater sin." From then on Pilate tried to release him, but the Jews cried out, "If you release this man, you are no friend of the emperor. Everyone who claims to be a king sets himself against the emperor."

When Pilate heard these words, he brought Jesus outside and sat on the judge's bench at a place called The Stone Pavement, or in Hebrew Gabbatha. Now it was the day of Preparation for the Passover; and it was about noon. He said to the Jews,

"Here is your King!" They cried out, "Away with him! Away with him! Crucify him!" Pilate asked them, "Shall I crucify your King?" The chief priests answered, "We have no king but the emperor." Then he handed him over to them to be crucified.

So they took Jesus; and carrying the cross by himself, he went out to what is called The Place of the Skull, which in Hebrew is called Golgotha. There they crucified him, and with him two others, one on either side, with Jesus between them. Pilate also had an inscription written and put on the cross. It read, "Jesus of Nazareth, the King of the Jews." Many of the Jews read this inscription, because the place where Jesus was crucified was near the city; and it was written in Hebrew, in Latin, and in Greek. Then the chief priests of the Jews said to Pilate, "Do not write, 'The King of the Jews,' but, 'This man said, I am King of the Jews.'" Pilate answered, "What I have written I have written." When the soldiers had crucified Jesus, they took his clothes and divided them into four parts, one for each soldier. They also took his tunic; now the tunic was seamless, woven in one piece from the top. So they said to one another, "Let us not tear it, but cast lots for it to see who will get it." This was to fulfill what the scripture says, "They divided my clothes among themselves, and for my clothing they cast lots." And that is what the soldiers did. Meanwhile, standing near the cross of Jesus were his mother, and his mother's sister, Mary the wife of Clopas, and Mary Magdalene. When Jesus saw his mother and the disciple whom he loved standing beside her, he said to his mother, "Woman, here is your son." Then he said to the disciple, "Here is your mother." And from that hour the disciple took her into his own home.

After this, when Jesus knew that all was now finished, he said (in order to fulfill the scripture), "I am thirsty." A jar full of sour wine was standing there. So they put a sponge full of the wine on a branch of hyssop and held it to his mouth. When Jesus had received the wine, he said, "It is finished." Then he bowed his head and gave up his spirit.

Since it was the day of Preparation, the Jews did not want the bodies left on the cross during the Sabbath, especially because that Sabbath was a day of great solemnity. So they asked Pilate to have the legs of the crucified men broken and the bodies removed. Then the soldiers came and broke the legs of the first and of the other who had been crucified with him. But when they came to Jesus and saw that he was already dead, they did not break his legs. Instead, one of the soldiers pierced his side with a spear, and at once blood and water came out. (He who saw this has testified so that you also may believe. His testimony is true, and he knows that he tells the truth.) These things occurred so that the scripture might be fulfilled, "None of his bones shall be broken." And again another passage of scripture says, "They will look on the one whom they have pierced."

After these things, Joseph of Arimathea, who was a disciple of Jesus, though a secret one because of his fear of the Jews, asked Pilate to let him take away the body of Jesus. Pilate gave him permission; so he came and removed his body. Nicodemus, who had at first come to Jesus by night, also came, bringing a mixture of myrrh and aloes, weighing about a hundred pounds. They took the body of Jesus and wrapped it with the spices in linen cloths, according to the burial custom of the Jews. Now there was a garden in the place where he was crucified, and in the garden there was a new tomb in which no one had ever been laid. And so, because it was the Jewish day of Preparation, and the tomb was nearby, they laid Jesus there.

The precise origin of this beautiful prayer is not clear. The original Latin version has been attributed to several possible authors including Bernard of Clairvaux (1090-1153). Paul Gerhardt (1607-1676) took the Latin text and translated it into German in the seventeenth century. Regardless of the source, it is a beautiful prayer that captures the piety and love of Christ.

> What language can I borrow
>   To thank you, dearest friend,
> For this your dying sorrow,
>   Your mercy without end?
> Bind me to you forever,
>   Give courage from above;
> Let not my weakness sever
>   Your bond of lasting love.

Reynolds Price (1933-2011) was an American writer of poems, novels, short stories, and essays. He wrote his first novel, *A Long and Happy Life*, in 1962. He was James B. Duke Professor of English at Duke University in his home state of North Carolina. His interest in biblical scholarship is reflected in the poem, "Jerusalem—Calvary" and a related short story, "Long Night." As the "trough" in Bethlehem was "real," so is the hole for the cross on Golgotha. Price leans into the stark realness of the earthly life of Jesus.

> Beyond this aromatic Greek monk
> With the roll of toilet paper by his foot
> (You must pay him to stand here)—
> An Altar on legs, beneath it a disc,
> In the disc a hole.
>   If you've paid enough
> (He names no sum). He'll say as you crouch
> "Reach in. Golgotha.
> Hole for cross."
>   Beware.
> Eight empty inches, then live rock—
> Cooling mouth, still raw
> At the lip. One whole arm inserted
> Would reach dead center

Elie Wiesel (1928-2016) was a Jewish writer and a holocaust survivor. In May 1944, Wiesel, with his parents and a sister, was sent to Auschwitz. His mother and sister were killed upon arrival; his father died just a few weeks before he was liberated. In this classic passage from his book *Night* (1960), Wiesel describes the walk past the victims who were hung in the yard in the concentration camp. While Christians must be very careful when using a text by a Jewish author, the simple idea that God is found in the middle of the suffering is a powerful Good Friday theme.

> Then came the march past the victims. The two men were no longer alive. Their tongues were hanging out, swollen and bluish. But the third rope was still moving: the child, too light, was still breathing . . .
>
> And so he remained for more than half an hour, lingering between life and death, writhing before our eyes.
>
> And we were forced to look at him at close range. He was still alive when I passed him. His tongue was still red, his eyes not yet extinguished.
>
> Behind me, I heard the same man asking: "For God's sake, where is God?"
>
> And from within me, I heard a voice answer: "Where He is? This is where—hanging here from this gallows..."
>
> That night, the soup tasted of corpses.

The power of love from the masses is captured in this poem by César Abraham Vallejo Mendoza (1892-1938). It is called "Masses" and translated by Robert Bly. César Vallejo was born in Santiago de Chuco in Peru. From a poor background, he has become the best-known Peruvian poet.

> When the battle was over,
> and the fighter was dead, a man came toward him
> and said to him: "Do not die; I love you so!"
> But the corpse, it was sad! went on dying.
>
> And two came near, and told him again and again:
> "Do not leave us! Courage! Return to life!"
> But the corpse, it was sad! went on dying.
>
> Millions of persons stood around him,
> all speaking the same thing: "Stay here, brother!"
> But the corpse, it was sad! went on dying.
>
> Then all the men on earth
> stood around him; the corpse looked at them sadly,
> deeply moved;
> He sat up slowly,
> put his arms around the first man, started to walk . . .

THE GREAT VIGIL OF EASTER

Year A

Matthew 28:1-10

After the Sabbath, as the first day of the week was dawning, Mary Magdalene and the other Mary went to see the tomb. And suddenly there was a great earthquake; for an angel of the Lord, descending from heaven, came and rolled back the stone and sat on it. His appearance was like lightning, and his clothing white as snow. For fear of him the guards shook and became like dead men. But the angel said to the women, "Do not be afraid; I know that you are looking for Jesus who was crucified. He is not here; for he has been raised, as he said. Come, see the place where he lay. Then go quickly and tell his disciples, 'He has been raised from the dead, and indeed he is going ahead of you to Galilee; there you will see him.' This is my message for you." So they left the tomb quickly with fear and great joy, and ran to tell his disciples. Suddenly Jesus met them and said, "Greetings!" And they came to him, took hold of his feet, and worshiped him. Then Jesus said to them, "Do not be afraid; go and tell my brothers to go to Galilee; there they will see me."

Year B

Mark 16:1-8

When the Sabbath was over, Mary Magdalene, and Mary the mother of James, and Salome bought spices, so that they might go and anoint Jesus. And very early on the first day of the week, when the sun had risen, they went to the tomb. They had been saying to one another, "Who will roll away the stone for us from the entrance to the tomb?" When they looked up, they saw that the stone, which was very large, had already been rolled back. As they entered the tomb, they saw a young man, dressed in a white robe, sitting on the right side; and they were alarmed. But he said to them, "Do not be alarmed; you are looking for Jesus of Nazareth, who was crucified. He has been raised; he is not here. Look, there is the place they laid him. But go, tell his disciples and Peter that he is going ahead of you to Galilee; there you will see him, just as he told you." So they went out and fled from the tomb, for terror and amazement had seized them; and they said nothing to anyone, for they were afraid.

Year C

Luke 24:1-12

On the first day of the week, at early dawn, the women who had come with Jesus from Galilee came to the tomb, taking the spices that they had prepared. They found the stone rolled away from the tomb, but when they went in, they did not find the body. While they were perplexed about this, suddenly two men in dazzling clothes stood beside them. The women were terrified and bowed their faces to the ground, but the men said to them, "Why do you look for the living among the dead? He is not here, but has risen. Remember how he told you, while he was still in Galilee, that the Son of Man must be handed over to sinners, and be crucified, and on the third day rise again." Then they remembered his words, and returning from the tomb, they told all this to the eleven and to all the rest. Now it was Mary Magdalene, Joanna, Mary the mother of James, and the other women with them who told this to the apostles. But these words seemed to them an idle tale, and they did not believe them. But Peter got up and ran to the tomb; stooping and looking in, he saw the linen cloths by themselves; then he went home, amazed at what had happened.

All the selections below reflect on the themes of the Resurrection.

R.S. Thomas (1913-2000) was a dour Welsh poet. His writing often reflected the Welsh terrain. "Via Negativa" is an invitation to learn that God is not a "thing" and that we need to recognize the vastness of God, which cannot be limited by our human understanding. God is an energetic absence which haunts all our lives.

Why no! I never thought other than
That God is that great absence
In our lives, the empty silence
Within, the place where we go
Seeking, not in hope to
Arrive or find. He keeps the interstices
In our knowledge, the darkness
Between stars. His are the echoes
We follow, the footprints he has just
Left. We put our hands in
His side hoping to find
It warm. We look at people
And places as though he had looked
At them, too; but miss the reflection.

Rowan Williams (b. 1950) is a distinguished theologian and preacher. In this sermon called "I do not know the man" (based on the text from Matthew 26:74), Williams reflects on the human capacity to distance ourselves from the demands of the gospel. He culminates with this excerpt, alluding right at the end to the words of Bach's St. Matthew Passion.

I shall never know him. There is always more than I can say or think, and when I believe I have understood him, he will turn and look out of such silence that I'll know I have still known nothing. Of course, he goes alone to his death, because we shall not know what it is for him to accept, and live his way into that great breach with the source of his life, which he calls "Father." I do not know him; all I have known is the stirring of a knowledge that in his silence and his death all men and women will find themselves free. I do not need to know him, to master him and categorize and theologize him, only to know that my life is to be found there. I do not know the man; I want to be where he is; I want to escape; I want his love; I want his absolution. I want to live, and I am afraid when he tells me I must learn to be mortal. I want the questions to stop.

And he went out and wept bitterly.

Erbarne dich, mein Gott...
Have mercy, Lord, on me,
For my tears' sake, forgive;
See, here, my heart and eyes
Grieve bitterly before thee.
Have mercy

Iris Murdoch (1919-1999), the philosopher and novelist, had the gift of capturing the moments of transformation and liberation of the self. In her novel *The Red and the Green*, the chaotic Barney—living with his sense of failure as an academic, a host of sexual inadequacies, a private journal full of self-pity and self-justification—discovers that transformation comes through a recognition that he is not the center of the world. Instead, he must learn not to control, to be empty, and surrender. The transformation from cross to empty tomb occurs at the Easter Mass.

> Barney went to the Easter Mass like a sleepwalker. He had decided on the previous day to go and now went automatically. Then quite suddenly, as if someone had come into the room and lightly touched him as he sat absent-mindedly, he was reminded of where he was and what occasion was being honoured. He recalled his good resolutions of three days ago when he had decided to simplify his life and make peace with Kathleen. Had that been mere meaningless emotion or had it been truly the pressure of another world upon his darkness? He remembered how he had felt sunk in himself beyond the possibility of change. [Then as he participated in the Easter Mass, Barney mused on why on most occasions he found the service disappointing.] ...
>
> Mary Magdalene might indeed have glimpsed Him in the garden somewhere, but for the rest of us there remained only the empty tomb. "He is not here." The Christ who travels towards Jerusalem and suffers there can be made into a familiar. The risen Christ is something

suddenly unknown. This metamorphosis had always in the past represented for Barney simply a disappointment, like the ending of a play. He had never thought of it as a starting point. He thought of it so now for the first time; and, with this shift of view, it became clear to him, with a sudden authoritative clarity, that it was the risen Christ and not the suffering Christ who must be his saviour: the absent Christ hidden in God and not that all too recognizable victim. He was too horribly, too intimately connected with his own degraded image of the Christ of Good Friday. Easter must purge that imagery now. The scourged tormented flesh appealed to something in him that was too grossly human since he had not the gift of compassion. These sufferings ended for him in self-pity and further on and shamefully in pleasure. This could not alter him a jot though he contemplated it forever. What was required of him was something which lay quite outside the deeply worked pattern of suffering, the plain possibility of change without drama and even without punishment. Perhaps after all that was the message of Easter. Absence not pain would be the rite of his salvation. As Barney walked home from Mass he also recalled to his mind events of yesterday which his visit to Rathblane had made him totally forget.

Ira Forest Stanphill (1914-1993) was born in New Mexico and became a famous American gospel music songwriter. He was a pastor working mainly in Assembly of God Churches. In this moving song, "I Know Who Holds Tomorrow," Stanphill captures the simple obligation of the Christian to trust in God and live day to day.

> I don't know about tomorrow
> I just live for day to day
> I don't borrow from the sunshine
> For its skies may turn to gray
>
> I don't worry o'er the future
> For I know what Jesus said
> And today I'll walk beside Him
> For He knows what lies ahead
>
> Many things about tomorrow
> I don't seem to understand
> But I know who holds tomorrow
> And I know who holds my hand
>
> Ev'ry step is getting brighter
> As the golden stairs I climb
> Ev'ry burden's getting lighter
> Ev'ry cloud is silver lined
>
> There the sun is always shining
> There no tear will dim the eye
> At the ending of the rainbow
> Where the mountains touch the sky
>
> Many things about tomorrow
> I don't seem to understand
> But I know who holds tomorrow
> And I know who holds my hand

EASTER DAY

John 20:1-18

Early on the first day of the week, while it was still dark, Mary Magdalene came to the tomb and saw that the stone had been removed from the tomb. So she ran and went to Simon Peter and the other disciple, the one whom Jesus loved, and said to them, "They have taken the Lord out of the tomb, and we do not know where they have laid him." Then Peter and the other disciple set out and went toward the tomb. The two were running together, but the other disciple outran Peter and reached the tomb first. He bent down to look in and saw the linen wrappings lying there, but he did not go in. Then Simon Peter came, following him, and went into the tomb. He saw the linen wrappings lying there, and the cloth that had been on Jesus' head, not lying with the linen wrappings but rolled up in a place by itself. Then the other disciple, who reached the tomb first, also went in, and he saw and believed; for as yet they did not understand the scripture, that he must rise from the dead. Then the disciples returned to their homes. But Mary stood weeping outside the tomb. As she wept, she bent over to look into the tomb; and she saw two angels in white, sitting where the body of Jesus had been lying, one at the head and the other at the feet. They said to her, "Woman, why are you weeping?" She said to them, "They have taken away my Lord, and I do not know where they have laid him." When she had said this, she turned around and saw Jesus standing there, but she did not know that it was Jesus. Jesus said to her, "Woman, why are you weeping? Whom are you looking for?" Supposing him to be the gardener, she said to him, "Sir, if you have carried him away, tell me where you have laid him, and I will take him away." Jesus said to her, "Mary!" She turned and said to him in Hebrew, "Rabbouni!" (which means Teacher). Jesus said to her, "Do not hold on to me, because I have not yet ascended to the Father. But go to my brothers and say to them, 'I am ascending to my Father and your Father, to my God and your God.'" Mary Magdalene went and announced to the disciples, "I have seen the Lord"; and she told them that he had said these things to her.

Maya Angelou (1928-2014) was a civil rights activist and poet. *I Know Why the Caged Bird Sings*, her autobiography, is a testament to her ability to overcome and to "sing" through her poems and other writings. What follows is her poem, "Touched by an Angel." For her Love conquers all, that Love which triumphs on Easter Day.

We, unaccustomed to courage
exiles from delight
live coiled in shells of loneliness
until love leaves its high holy temple
and comes into our sight
to liberate us into life.

Love arrives
and in its train come ecstasies
old memories of pleasure
ancient histories of pain.
Yet if we are bold,
love strikes away the chains of fear
from our souls.

We are weaned from our timidity
In the flush of love's light
we dare be brave
And suddenly we see
that love costs all we are
and will ever be.
Yet it is only love
which sets us free.

Rowan Williams (b. 1950), the retired Archbishop of Canterbury and now Master of Magdalene College, Cambridge, is a formidable expositor of theological themes. Here in his book *Resurrection: Interpreting the Easter Gospel*, he explains how resurrection contrasts with crucifixion. Resurrection is in many ways harder. In the Crucifixion, we can almost find comfort in the divine act of solidarity with suffering; in the Resurrection, we find the tomb empty and the invitation to re-encounter Christ and become an active agent in the work of bringing about the kingdom.

At each stage, I seek finality; my illusory wants return. Hence the phenomenon . . . the "unending flow back and forth between speech and silence," and hence the importance of the resurrection for our grasp of the nature of religious language. We have a language for Calvary, all too familiar a language: we are used to talking about suffering, ours and the world's, and we are tempted to rest content with speaking of a suffering God, whose infinite sympathy somehow makes the world's pain bearable or intelligible. The empty tomb silences us: the memory, the *monument*, of the Great Fellow-Sufferer vanishes. There is, it seems, more to be said; yet it is by no means clear what can be said. We rightly shrink from a hasty response to Easter morning which blandly says that Jesus, our God-in-Jesus, has triumphed over pain and death, has done with it, so that what seemed tragic is really not so. 'The absent Christ, hidden in God, may appear simply to witness to an ultimate separation between God and suffering. The empty tomb, then, is indeed a moment of inarticulacy, doubt, and even (as for the women of Mark

16) fear, of disorientation and the sense of abandonment ("They have taken away my Lord . . . ").

And when the risen Jesus appears, to give us back our speech, when the sense of meaningfulness and affirmation seizes us again, we are not asked to describe or systematize. The language given us is that of self-knowledge, penitence, and that of preaching and absolution: it is the language of *confession*, in the double sense of that word so richly exploited by Augustine. This is a language which maintains the possibility of stripping and questioning, and which lays bare to the world how this may be a process of self-recovery, and the creation of renewed relations. A language which stayed at Calvary would resolve the problem of suffering passively; while the language of Easter is inextricably bound up with the practice of the Church, in prayer and mission alike. In one way, it leaves Calvary a greater problem than ever, but it also affirms that it is not a problem whose resolution is in words—even words about the suffering of a compassionate God.

"The Wreck of the Deutschland" is a long poem written by Gerard Manley Hopkins (1844-1889). The English poet was agonizing over the loss of 168 lives on the German ship, Deutschland, which was shipwrecked on the beaches of the Kentish Knock at the mouth of the Thames River in England. As Jesus calmed the waters of the lake at Gennesareth when the disciples were frightened, so Hopkins looks for the Christ in "The Wreck of the Deutschland." Jesus is present in danger and in the hour of death. For Hopkins, Jesus is ever "eastering" in us, bringing new life beyond the grave.

> Thou mastering me
> God! giver of breath and bread;
> World's strand, sway of the sea;
> Lord of living and dead;
> Thou hast bound bones & veins in me, fastened me flesh,
> And after it almost unmade, what with dread,
> Thy doing: and dost thou touch me afresh?
> Over again I feel thy finger and find thee . . .
>
> Dame, at our door
> Drowned, and among our shoals,
> Remember us in the roads, the heaven-haven of the Reward:
> Our King back, Oh, upon English souls!
> Let him easter in us, be a dayspring to the dimness of us, be a crimson-cresseted east,
> More brightening her, rare-dear Britain, as his reign rolls,
> Pride, rose, prince, hero of us, high-priest,
> Our hearts' charity's hearth's fire, our thoughts' chivalry's throng's Lord.

Mary could not be far from Jesus in life or in death. She stood outside the tomb weeping for her beloved. From the tomb, Jesus came to her as he always had. She reached for the warmth of his beautiful body, but Jesus cautioned her: not this time I have not yet ascended. Go tell the others, Mary. Mary was the Church's first Easter preacher, the bearer of good news. A woman who hosted demons in her being now was host to the disciples when she made her confession: "I have seen the Lord." Malcolm Guite (b. 1957), poet and singer-songwriter, wrote a sonnet to remember this Easter eyewitness, "Mary Magdalene."

> Men called you light so as to load you down,
> And burden you with their own weight of sin,
> A woman forced to cover and contain
> Those seven devils sent by Everyman.
> But one man set you free and took your part
> One man knew and loved you to the core
> The broken alabaster of your heart
> Revealed to Him alone a hidden door,
> Into a garden where the fountain sealed,
> Could flow at last for him in healing tears,
> Till, in another garden, he revealed
> The perfect Love that cast out all your fears,
> And quickened you with love's own sway and swing,
> As light and lovely as the news you bring.

THE SECOND SUNDAY
OF EASTER

Year A, B, and C

John 20:19-31

When it was evening on that day, the first day of the week, and
the doors of the house where the disciples had met were locked
for fear of the Jews, Jesus came and stood among them and said,
"Peace be with you." After he said this, he showed them his hands
and his side. Then the disciples rejoiced when they saw the Lord.
Jesus said to them again, "Peace be with you. As the Father has
sent me, so I send you." When he had said this, he breathed on
them and said to them, "Receive the Holy Spirit. If you forgive
the sins of any, they are forgiven them; if you retain the sins of
any, they are retained." But Thomas (who was called the Twin),
one of the twelve, was not with them when Jesus came. So the
other disciples told him, "We have seen the Lord." But he said
to them, "Unless I see the mark of the nails in his hands, and put
my finger in the mark of the nails and my hand in his side, I will
not believe." A week later his disciples were again in the house,
and Thomas was with them. Although the doors were shut, Jesus came and stood among them and said, "Peace be with you."
Then he said to Thomas, "Put your finger here and see my hands.
Reach out your hand and put it in my side. Do not doubt but
believe." Thomas answered him, "My Lord and my God!" Jesus said to him, "Have you believed because you have seen me?
Blessed are those who have not seen and yet have come to be-

lieve." Now Jesus did many other signs in the presence of his disciples, which are not written in this book. But these are written so that you may come to believe that Jesus is the Messiah, the Son of God, and that through believing you may have life in his name."

The remarkable short story, "The Expert on God," by John L'Heureux (b. 1934), describes the predicament of a recently ordained priest whose faith is full of doubt. Skepticism abounds about everything from the Trinity to the presence of Christ in the Eucharist. After time, he suppresses his doubts, but one doubt remains about the love of God. The story reaches a climax on Christmas day. He notices a red sports car partially turned over on its side. He grabs his vial of holy oil and runs to the car where he seeks to offer the last rites. In this conclusion, the priest becomes the Mother Mary, cradling Jesus, as in the Pieta.

> He shook with an involuntary sob then, and as he did, the boy shuddered in agony and choked on the blood that had begun to pour from his mouth. The priest could see death beginning to ease across the boy's face. And still he could say nothing.
>
> The boy turned some dying reflex and his head tilted in the priest's arms, trusting, like a lover. And at once the priest, faithless, unrepentant, gave up his prayers and bent to him and whispered, fierce and burning, "I love you," and continued till there was no breath, "I love you. I love you. I love you."

In the award-winning play, *Doubt: A Parable,* by John Patrick Shanley (b. 1950), later adapted into an Oscar-nominated film starring Meryl Streep and Philip Seymour Hoffman, a sexual misconduct accusation threatens to bring down the newly-installed Father Flynn of St. Nicolas Church School in New York. His chief attacker is the stalwart Sister Aloysius, who ruthlessly challenges him, certain of her convictions about him without concrete proof. The play's subtitle "A Parable" is apt, as in its opening words, Flynn preaches a homily about the perils and possibilities of doubt itself.

> What do you do when you're not sure? That is the topic of my sermon today. Last year, when President Kennedy was assassinated, who among us did not experience the most profound disorientation? Despair? Which way? What now? What do I say to my kids? What do I tell myself? It was a time of people sitting together, bound together by a common feeling of hopelessness. But think of that! Your BOND with your fellow being was your Despair. It was a public experience. It was awful, but we were in it together. How much worse is it then for the lone man, the lone woman, stricken by a private calamity? "No one knows I'm sick." "No one knows I've lost my last real friend." "No one knows I've done something wrong." Imagine the isolation. Now you see the world as through a window. On one side of the glass: happy, untroubled people, and on the other side: you. I want to tell you a story. A cargo ship sank one night. It caught fire and went down. And only this one sailor survived. He found a lifeboat, rigged a sail . . . and being of a nautical discipline . . . turned his

eyes to the Heavens and read the stars. He set a course for his home, and exhausted, fell asleep. Clouds rolled in. And for the next twenty nights, he could no longer see the stars. He thought he was on course, but there was no way to be certain. And as the days rolled on, and the sailor wasted away, he began to have doubts. Had he set his course right? Was he still going on towards his home? Or was he horribly lost . . . and doomed to a terrible death? No way to know. The message of the constellations—had he imagined it because of his desperate circumstance? Or had he seen truth once . . . and now had to hold on to it without further reassurance? There are those of you in church today who know exactly the crisis of faith I describe. And I want to say to you: doubt can be a bond as powerful and sustaining as certainty. When you are lost, you are not alone.

George Herbert (1593-1633)—poet and priest—wrote this extraordinary meditation about God and entitled it simply "Love." There is a gentleness in the interaction of love with humanity. And the poem culminates in a meditation on the Eucharist, where love is ingested and taken into the body.

Love bade me welcome. Yet my soul drew back
Guilty of dust and sin.
But quick-eyed Love, observing me grow slack
From my first entrance in,
Drew nearer to me, sweetly questioning,
If I lacked anything.
A guest, I answered, worthy to be here:
Love said, You shall be he.
I the unkind, ungrateful? Ah my dear,
I cannot look on thee.
Love took my hand, and smiling did reply,
Who made the eyes but I?
Truth Lord, but I have marred them: let my shame
Go where it doth deserve.
And know you not, says Love, who bore the blame?
My dear, then I will serve.
You must sit down, says Love, and taste my meat:
So I did sit and eat.

It must have been a glorious day when the Risen Lord stood with fearful disciples and gently said: "Peace be with you." Jesus, who had fished with them, gave them the ultimate gift, the gift of the Holy Spirit. We sing "It is well with my soul." We sing "I've got peace like a river." Paul Simon's "Peace Like a River" is a ballad that hauntingly captures "Peace be with you." In this song, Paul Simon is inviting us to be authentically ourselves and to transcend the "group think" mentality that seeks to batter us to look at the world in a certain way. The promise of the Resurrection is a peace that equally transcends the ephemeral and the immediate.

THE THIRD SUNDAY
OF EASTER

Year A

Luke 24:13-35

Now on that same day two of Jesus' disciples were going to a village called Emmaus, about seven miles from Jerusalem, and talking with each other about all these things that had happened. While they were talking and discussing, Jesus himself came near and went with them, but their eyes were kept from recognizing him. And he said to them, "What are you discussing with each other while you walk along?" They stood still, looking sad. Then one of them, whose name was Cleopas, answered him, "Are you the only stranger in Jerusalem who does not know the things that have taken place there in these days?" He asked them, "What things?" They replied, "The things about Jesus of Nazareth, who was a prophet mighty in deed and word before God and all the people, and how our chief priests and leaders handed him over to be condemned to death and crucified him. But we had hoped that he was the one to redeem Israel. Yes, and besides all this, it is now the third day since these things took place. Moreover, some women of our group astounded us. They were at the tomb early this morning, and when they did not find his body there, they came back and told us that they had indeed seen a vision of angels who said that he was alive. Some of those who were with us went to the tomb and found it just as the women had said; but they did not see him." Then he said to them, "Oh, how foolish you are, and how slow of heart to believe all that the prophets have declared! Was it not necessary that the Messiah should suffer these things and then enter into his glory?" Then beginning with Moses and all the prophets, he interpreted to them the things about himself in all the scriptures. As they came near the village to which they were going, he walked ahead as if he were going on. But they urged him strongly, saying, "Stay with us, because it is almost evening and the day is now nearly over." So he went in to stay with them. When he was at the table with them, he took bread, blessed and broke it, and gave it to them. Then their eyes were opened, and they recognized him; and he vanished from their sight. They said to each other, "Were not our hearts burning within us while he was talking to us on the road, while he was opening the scriptures to us?" That same hour they got up and returned to Jerusalem; and they found the eleven and their companions gathered together. They were saying, "The Lord has risen indeed, and he has appeared to Simon!" Then they told what had happened on the road, and how he had been made known to them in the breaking of the bread.

Year B

Luke 24:36b-48

Jesus himself stood among the disciples and said to them, "Peace be with you." They were startled and terrified, and thought that they were seeing a ghost. He said to them, "Why are you frightened, and why do doubts arise in your hearts? Look at my hands and my feet; see that it is I myself. Touch me and see; for a ghost does not have flesh and bones as you see that I have." And when he had said this, he showed them his hands and his feet. While in their joy they were disbelieving and still wondering, he said to them, "Have you anything here to eat?" They gave him a piece of broiled fish, and he took it and ate in their presence. Then he said to them, "These are my words that I spoke to you while I was still with you—that everything written about me in the law of Moses, the prophets, and the psalms must be fulfilled." Then he opened their minds to understand the scriptures, and he said to them, "Thus it is written, that the Messiah is to suffer and to rise from the dead on the third day, and that repentance and forgiveness of sins is to be proclaimed in his name to all nations, beginning from Jerusalem. You are witnesses of these things."

Year C

John 21:1-19

Jesus showed himself again to the disciples by the Sea of Tiberius; and he showed himself in this way. Gathered there together were Simon Peter, Thomas called the Twin, Nathanael of Cana in Galilee, the sons of Zebedee, and two others of his disciples. Simon Peter said to them, "I am going fishing." They said to him, "We will go with you." They went out and got into the boat, but that night they caught nothing. Just after daybreak, Jesus stood on the beach; but the disciples did not know that it was Jesus. Jesus said to them, "Children, you have no fish, have you?" They answered him, "No." He said to them, "Cast the net to the right side of the boat, and you will find some." So they cast it, and now they were not able to haul it in because there were so many fish. That disciple whom Jesus loved said to Peter, "It is the Lord!" When Simon Peter heard that it was the Lord, he put on some clothes, for he was naked, and jumped into the sea. But the other disciples came in the boat, dragging the net full of fish, for they were not far from the land, only about a hundred yards off. When they had gone ashore, they saw a charcoal fire there, with fish on it, and bread. Jesus said to them, "Bring some of the fish that you have just caught." So Simon Peter went aboard and hauled the net ashore, full of large fish, a hundred fifty-three of them; and though there were so many, the net was not torn. Jesus said to them, "Come and have breakfast." Now none of the disciples dared to ask him, "Who are you?" because they knew it was the Lord. Jesus came and took the bread and gave it to them, and did the same with the fish. This was now the third time that Jesus appeared to the disciples after he was raised from the dead. When they had finished breakfast, Jesus said to Simon Peter, "Simon son of John, do you love me more than these?" He said to him, "Yes, Lord; you know that I love you." Jesus said to him, "Feed my lambs." A second time he said to him, "Simon son of John, do you love me?" He said to him, "Yes, Lord; you know that I love you." Jesus said to him, "Tend my sheep." He said to him the third time, "Simon son of John, do you love me?" Peter felt hurt because he said to him the third time, "Do you love me?" And he said to him, "Lord, you know everything; you know that I love you." Jesus said to him, "Feed my sheep. Very truly, I tell you, when you were younger, you used to fasten your own belt and to go wherever you wished. But when you grow old, you will stretch out your hands, and someone else will fasten a belt around you and take you where you do not wish to go." (He said this to indicate the kind of death by which he would glorify God.) After this he said to him, "Follow me."

On the road to Emmaus, we have two disciples trying to make sense of the mystery of the Incarnation. What exactly has happened here? Denise Levertov (1923-1997) was a British-born American poet. Her mother was Welsh, and her father was raised a Hasidic Jew but converted to Christianity and became an Anglican priest. She was part of the Black Mountain (North Carolina) group of poets and was an important voice in the American avant-garde. In the 1960s Levertov was well known for her activism and feminism. For her, the Christian mystery of the incarnation is entrusted to us in the Eternal Word.

> It's when we face for a moment
> the worst our kind can do, and shudder to know
> the taint in our own selves, that awe
> cracks the mind's shell and enters the heart:
> not to a flower, not to a dolphin,
> to no innocent form
> but to this creature vainly sure
> it and no other is god-like, God
> (out of compassion for our ugly
> failure to evolve) entrusts,
> as guest, as brother, the Word.

In Luke, the materiality of Jesus is an issue. Wendell Berry (b. 1934) is a farmer, poet, and environmental activist. In this poem, we see Berry the theologian at work. It starts with almost a pantheistic affirmation of the disclosure of God in nature and then moves to the Word (note the capital) which alludes to the Christ of scripture who is involved in creation.

> In the April rain I climbed up to drink
> of the live water leaping off the hill,
> white over the rocks. Where the mossy root
> of a sycamore cups the flow, I drank
> and saw the branches feathered with green.
> The thickets, I said, send up their praise
> at dawn. Was that what I meant—I meant
> my words to have the heft and grace, the flight
> and weight of the very hill, its life
> rising—or was it some old exultation
> that abides with me? We'll not soon escape
> the faith of our fathers—no more than
> crazy old Mrs. Gaines, whom my grandmother
> remembers standing balanced eighty years ago
> atop a fence in Port Royal, Kentucky,
> singing: "One Lord, one Faith, and one
> Cornbread." They had a cage built for her
> in a room, "nearly as big as the room, not
> cramped up," and when she grew wild
> they kept her there. But mostly she went free
> in the town, and they allowed the children
> to go for walks with her. She strayed once
> beyond where they thought she went, was lost
> to them, "and they had an awful time

finding her." For her, to be free
was only to be lost. What is it about her
that draws me on, so that my mind becomes a child
to follow after her? An old woman
when my grandmother was a girl, she must have seen
the virgin forest standing here, the amplitude
of our beginning, of which no speech
remains. Out of the town's lost history,
buried in minds long buried, she has come,
brought back by a memory near death. I see her
in her dusky clothes, hair uncombed, the children
following. I see her wandering, muttering
to herself as her way was, among these hills
half a century before my birth, in the silence
of such speech as i know. Dawn and twilight
and dawn again trembling in the leaves
over her, she tramped the raveling verges
of her time. It was a shadowy country
that she knew, holding a darkness that was past
and a darkness to come. The fleeting lights
tattered her churchly speech to mad song.
When her poor wandering head broke the confines
of all any of them knew, they put her in a cage.
But I am glad to know it was a commodious cage,
not cramped up. And I am glad to know
that other times the town left her free
to be as she was in it, and to go her way.
May it abide a poet with as much grace!
For I too am perhaps a little mad,
standing here wet in the drizzle, listening

to the clashing syllables of the water. Surely
there is a great Word being put together here.
I begin to hear it gather in the opening
of the flowers and the leafing-out of the trees,
in the growth of bird nests in the crotches
of the branches, in the settling of the dead
leaves into the ground, in the whittling
of beetle and grub, in my thoughts
moving in the hill's flesh. Coming here,
I crossed a place where a stream flows
underground, and the sounds of the hidden water
and the water come to light braided in my ear.
I think the maker is here, creating his hill
as it will be, out of what it was.
The thickets, I say, send up their praise
at dawn! One Lord, one Faith, and one Cornbread
forever! But hush. Wait. Be as still
as the dead and the unborn in whose silence
that old one walked, muttering and singing,
followed by the children.
For a time there
I turned away from the words I knew, and was lost.
For a time I was lost and free, speechless
in the multitudinous assembling of his Word.

After all that had happened to Peter, the concluding words of the Johannine beach breakfast from Jesus are "follow me." In the short story, "The Welcome Table," Alice Walker contrasts the offer to follow Jesus with the hostility of the church members who refuse to welcome the old lady.

The old woman stood with eyes uplifted in her Sunday-go-to meeting clothes: high shoes polished about the tops and toes, a long rusty dress adorned with an old corsage, long withered, and the remnants of an elegant silk scarf as headrag stained with grease from the many oily pigtails underneath. Perhaps she had known suffering. There was a dazed and sleepy look in her aged blue-brown eyes. But for those who searched hastily for "reasons" in that old tight face, shut now like an ancient door, there was nothing to be read. And so they gazed nakedly upon their own fear transferred; a fear of the black and the old, a terror of the unknown as well as of the deeply known. Some of those who saw her there on the church steps spoke words about her that were hardly fit to be heard, others held their pious peace; and some felt vague stirrings of pity, small and persistent and hazy, as if she were an old collie turned out to die . . .

Still she had come down the road toward the big white church alone. Just herself, an old forgetful woman, nearly blind with age. Just her and her eyes raised dully to the glittering cross that crowned the sheer silver steeple. She had walked along the road in a stagger from her house a half mile away. Perspiration, cold and clammy, stood on her brow and along the creases by her thin wasted nose. She stopped to calm herself on the wide front steps, not looking about her as they might have expected her to do, but simply standing quite still, except for a slight quivering of her throat and tremors that shook her cotton-stockinged legs.

The reverend of the church stopped her pleasantly as she stepped into the vestibule. Did he say, as they thought he did, kindly, "Auntie, you know this is not your church?" As if one could choose the wrong one. But no one remembers, for they never spoke of it afterward, and she brushed past him anyway, as if she had been brushing past him all her life, except this time she was in a hurry. Inside the church she sat on the very first bench from the back, gazing with concentration at the stained-glass window over her head. It was cold, even inside the church, and she was shivering. Everybody could see. They stared at her as they came in and sat down near the front. It was cold, very cold to them, too; outside the church it was below freezing and not much above inside. But the sight of her, sitting there somehow passionately ignoring them, brought them up short, burning . . .

The old woman stood at the top of the steps looking about in bewilderment. She had been singing in her head. They had interrupted her. Promptly she began to sing again, though this time a sad song. Suddenly, however, she looked down the long gray highway and saw something interesting and delightful coming. She started to grin, toothlessly, with short giggles of joy, jumping about and slapping her hands on her knees. And soon it became apparent why she was so happy. For coming down the highway at a firm though leisurely pace was Jesus. He was wearing an immaculate white, long dress trimmed in gold around the neck and hem, and a red, a bright red, cape. Over his left arm he carried a brilliant blue blanket. He was wearing sandals and a beard and he had long brown hair parted on the right side. His eyes, brown, had wrinkles around them as if he smiled or looked at the sun a lot. She would have known him, recognized him, anywhere. There was a sad but joyful look to his face, like a candle was glowing behind it, and he walked with sure even steps in her direction, as if he were walking on the sea. Except that he was not carrying in his arms a baby sheep, he looked exactly like the picture of him that she had hanging over her bed at home. She had taken it out of a white lady's Bible while she was working for her. She had looked at that picture for more years than she could remember, but never once had she really expected to see him. She squinted her eyes to be sure he wasn't carrying a little sheep in one arm, but he was not. Ecstatically she began to wave her arms for fear he would miss seeing her, for he walked looking straight ahead on the shoulder of the highway, and from time to time looking upward at the sky.

All he said when he got up close to her was "Follow me," and she bounded down to his side with all the bob and speed of one so old. For every one of his long determined steps she made two quick ones. They walked along in deep silence for a long time. Finally she started telling him about how many years she had cooked for them, cleaned for them, nursed them. He looked at her kindly but in silence. She told him indignantly about how they had grabbed her when she was singing in her head and not looking, and how they had tossed her out of his church. A old heifer like me, she said, straightening up next to Jesus, breathing hard. But he smiled down at her and she felt better instantly and time just seemed to fly by. When they passed her house, forlorn and sagging, weather-beaten and patched, by the side of the road, she did not even notice it, she was so happy to be out walking along the highway with Jesus.

She broke the silence once more to tell Jesus how glad she was that he had come, how she had often looked at his picture hanging on her wall (she hoped he didn't know she had stolen it) over her bed, and how she had never expected to see him down here in person. Jesus gave her one of his beautiful smiles and they walked on. She did not know where they were going; someplace wonderful, she suspected. The ground was like clouds under their feet, and she felt she could walk forever without becoming the least bit tired. She even began to sing out loud some of the old spirituals she loved, but she didn't want to annoy Jesus, who looked so thoughtful, so she quieted down. They walked on, looking straight over the treetops into the sky, and the smiles that played over her dry wind-cracked face were like first clean ripples across a stagnant pond. On they walked without stopping.

At Vatican II, in *Dei Verbum* (the Word of God—November 18, 1965), the Roman Catholic Church talks about offering to the faithful "the bread of life from the table both of God's word and of Christ's body." It is an invitation to get to know Christ both through the Eucharist and through scripture.

(21.) The Church has always venerated the divine Scriptures just as she venerates the body of the Lord, since, especially in the sacred liturgy, she unceasingly receives and offers to the faithful the bread of life from the table both of God's word and of Christ's body. She has always maintained them, and continues to do so, together with sacred tradition, as the supreme rule of faith, since, as inspired by God and committed once and for all to writing, they impart the word of God Himself without change, and make the voice of the Holy Spirit resound in the words of the prophets and Apostles. Therefore, like the Christian religion itself, all the preaching of the Church must be nourished and regulated by Sacred Scripture. For in the sacred books, the Father who is in heaven meets His children with great love and speaks with them; and the force and power in the word of God is so great that it stands as the support and energy of the Church, the strength of faith for her sons, the food of the soul, the pure and everlasting source of spiritual life. Consequently these words are perfectly applicable to Sacred Scripture: "For the word of God is living and active" (Heb. 4:12) and "it has power to build you up and give you your heritage among all those who are sanctified" (Acts 20:32; see 1 Thess. 2:13).

(22.) Easy access to Sacred Scripture should be provided for all the Christian faithful. That is why the Church from the very beginning accepted as her own that very ancient Greek translation of the Old Testament which is called the septuagint; and she has always given a place of honor to other Eastern translations and Latin ones especially the Latin translation known as the vulgate. But since the word of God should be accessible at all times, the Church by her authority and with maternal concern sees to it that suitable and correct translations are made into different languages, especially from the original texts of the sacred books. And should the opportunity arise and the Church authorities approve, if these translations are produced in cooperation with the separated brethren as well, all Christians will be able to use them.

(23.) The bride of the incarnate Word, the Church taught by the Holy Spirit, is concerned to move ahead toward a deeper understanding of the Sacred Scriptures so that she may increasingly feed her sons with the divine words. Therefore, she also encourages the study of the holy Fathers of both East and West and of sacred liturgies. Catholic exegetes then and other students of sacred theology, working diligently together and using appropriate means, should devote their energies, under the watchful care of the sacred teaching office of the Church, to an exploration and exposition of the divine writings. This should be so done that as many ministers of the divine word as possible will be able effectively to provide the nourishment of the Scriptures for the people of God, to enlighten their minds, strengthen their wills, and set men's hearts on fire with the love of God. (1) The sacred synod encourages the sons of the Church and Biblical scholars to continue energetically, following the mind of the Church, with the work they have so well begun, with a constant renewal of vigor. (2)

(24.) Sacred theology rests on the written word of God, together with sacred tradition, as its primary and perpetual foundation. By scrutinizing in the light of faith all truth stored up in the mystery of Christ, theology is most powerfully strengthened and constantly rejuvenated by that word. For the Sacred Scriptures contain the word of God and since they are inspired, really are the word of God; and so the study of the sacred page is, as it were, the soul of sacred theology. (3) By the same word of Scripture the ministry of the word also, that is, pastoral preaching, catechetics and all Christian instruction, in which the liturgical homily must hold the foremost place, is nourished in a healthy way and flourishes in a holy way.

THE FOURTH SUNDAY
OF EASTER

John 10:1-10

Jesus said, "Very truly, I tell you, anyone who does not enter the sheepfold by the gate but climbs in by another way is a thief and a bandit. The one who enters by the gate is the shepherd of the sheep. The gatekeeper opens the gate for him, and the sheep hear his voice. He calls his own sheep by name and leads them out. When he has brought out all his own, he goes ahead of them, and the sheep follow him because they know his voice. They will not follow a stranger, but they will run from him because they do not know the voice of strangers." Jesus used this figure of speech with them, but they did not understand what he was saying to them. So again Jesus said to them, "Very truly, I tell you, I am the gate for the sheep. All who came before me are thieves and bandits; but the sheep did not listen to them. I am the gate. Whoever enters by me will be saved, and will come in and go out and find pasture. The thief comes only to steal and kill and destroy. I came that they may have life, and have it abundantly."

Year B

John 10:11-18

Jesus said, "I am the good shepherd. The good shepherd lays down his life for the sheep. The hired hand, who is not the shepherd and does not own the sheep, sees the wolf coming and leaves the sheep and runs away—and the wolf snatches them and scatters them. The hired hand runs away because a hired hand does not care for the sheep. I am the good shepherd. I know my own and my own know me, just as the Father knows me and I know the Father. And I lay down my life for the sheep. I have other sheep that do not belong to this fold. I must bring them also, and they will listen to my voice. So there will be one flock, one shepherd. For this reason the Father loves me, because I lay down my life in order to take it up again. No one takes it from me, but I lay it down of my own accord. I have power to lay it down, and I have power to take it up again. I have received this command from my Father."

Year C

John 10:22-30

At that time the festival of the Dedication took place in Jerusalem. It was winter, and Jesus was walking in the temple, in the portico of Solomon. So the Jews gathered around him and said to him, "How long will you keep us in suspense? If you are the Messiah, tell us plainly." Jesus answered, "I have told you, and you do not believe. The works that I do in my Father's name testify to me; but you do not believe, because you do not belong to my sheep. My sheep hear my voice. I know them, and they follow me. I give them eternal life, and they will never perish. No one will snatch them out of my hand. What my Father has given me is greater than all else, and no one can snatch it out of the Father's hand. The Father and I are one."

All the selections apply to all of the gospel readings.

The opening extract is from St. Gregory the Great (c. 540-604). In this famous homily, St. Gregory invites us to focus on the pastures in which the sheep are being cared for by the shepherd. The pastures are the anticipation of heaven that we can enjoy here on earth. It is an invitation to a deep joy, where we are not distracted by the charms of prosperity.

Christ the Good Shepherd

So the sheep find the Lord's pastures; for anyone who follows him with an undivided heart is nourished in a pasture which is forever green. What are the pastures of these sheep if they are not the deepest joys of the everlasting fresh pastures of paradise? For the pasture of the saints is to see God face to face; when the vision of God never fails, the soul receives its fill of the food of life for ever.

And so, dear brethren, let us seek these pastures and there join in the joy and the celebrations of so many citizens of heaven. Let their happiness and rejoicing be an invitation to us. Let our hearts grow warm, brethren, let our faith be rekindled, let our desires for heavenly things grow warm; for to love like this is to be on the way.

No misfortune should distract us from this happiness and deep joy; for if anyone is anxious to reach a destination, the roughness of the road will not make him change his mind. The charms of prosperity must not lead us astray; for only a foolish traveler, when he sees pleasant fields on his way, forgets to go on towards his destination.

The sheep theme is the great metaphor for ministry. Hilary Peter Frank Greenwood (1929-2003) was a priest, a British theologian, and a member of the Anglican religious order The Society of Sacred Mission. Greenwood reflects in this poem "Knotty Nineties" on what exactly he felt ministry involved.

What I like about being a priest
is nothing to do with the cultic beast
or having a message to write on the leaves
or offering charms to the heart that grieves
or counting the sheep in a pitch-pine fold
or wearing a shirt of cloth-of-gold,
no, none of these—but marrying
the glory to the little thing:
to eavesdrop on a monologue
delivered to a woolly dog;
to hear the tones of righteous rage
excite the prophet of schoolboy age;
to sit down in a bus behind
four lots of fingers intertwined;
to see the boy's face in the man's
blush when he comes to put up the banns:
to watch rheumatic ladies pat
a blessing on the pampered cat—
what I like about being a priest
is turning everything to the east.

In each of the Gospels for this fourth Sunday in Easter, Jesus is found protecting his flock, the fledgling Church. He is the gate to them; he is the good shepherd; and he is the Messiah who gives to his sheep eternal life for "the Father and he are one." Ralph Vaughan Williams set William Blake's poem to music in his 1958 song cycle *Ten Blake Songs*. Do not miss that Blake's shepherd "follows his sheep all the day . . . " Follows, not leads! William Blake (1757-1827) is best known for his *Songs of Innocence*. He was a poet of England's Romantic Age and some say the greatest artist Britain has ever produced.

> How sweet is the Shepherd's sweet lot
> From the morn to the evening he strays;
> He shall follow his sheep all the day,
> And his tongue shall be filled with praise.
>
> For he hears the lamb's innocent call,
> And he hears the ewe's tender reply;
> He is watchful while they are in peace,
> For they know when their Shepherd is nigh.

In Easter, it is not surprising that we are hearing of one shepherd for one flock. There has always been a yearning for the Body of Christ, the Church, to be one. The Indian Evangelist, Sundar Singh (1889-1929), taught and preached in parables. One such parable deals with "One Fold and One Shepherd."

A German gentleman who was an interested supporter of missions asked me, "What form of Church organization will be adopted if all India becomes Christian?" I replied; "There is no country in the world that is wholly Christian and there never will be, and even if India ever becomes Christian, it will be only the extent that any of the countries of the West are Christian. For as long as the world lasts, good and bad, and earnest and indifferent, will always be found. Only if all were changed in heart and life could we say that the Kingdom of heaven had come, but then the world would not be world, it would be heaven."

About the Church: people are continually introducing changes in worship and creating new sects, but they are not satisfied with any of them. The real need is not that we should adopt new forms, but that through the Living Christ, rivers of living water should begin to flow through us. When the water of a Himalayan mountain stream reaches the plains men dig canals for it; but away among the great mountains it makes its own way past cliff, and rock and valley, and no one digs a channel for it. So the new life at first snakes its way through the lives of individual Christians but they feel no need of organizing channels for it, but when it flows through whole communities, then they will organize channels, or churches, for it to meet their needs. At that time, the man-made sects will disappear, and there will be only one Church of the Living Christ, and there shall be "one fold and one shepherd." (John 10:6)

THE FIFTH SUNDAY
OF EASTER

Year A

John 14:1-14

Jesus said, "Do not let your hearts be troubled. Believe in God, believe also in me. In my Father's house there are many dwelling places. If it were not so, would I have told you that I go to prepare a place for you? And if I go and prepare a place for you, I will come again and will take you to myself, so that where I am, there you may be also. And you know the way to the place where I am going." Thomas said to him, "Lord, we do not know where you are going. How can we know the way?" Jesus said to him, "I am the way, and the truth, and the life. No one comes to the Father except through me. If you know me, you will know my Father also. From now on you do know him and have seen him." Philip said to him, "Lord, show us the Father, and we will be satisfied." Jesus said to him, "Have I been with you all this time, Philip, and you still do not know me? Whoever has seen me has seen the Father. How can you say, 'Show us the Father'? Do you not believe that I am in the Father and the Father is in me? The words that I say to you I do not speak on my own; but the Father who dwells in me does his works. Believe me that I am in the Father and the Father is in me; but if you do not, then believe me because of the works themselves. Very truly, I tell you, the one who believes in me will also do the works that I do and, in fact, will do greater works than these, because I am going to the Father. I will do whatever you ask in my name, so that the Father may be glorified in the Son. If in my name you ask me for anything, I will do it."

Year B

John 15:1-8

Jesus said to his disciples, "I am the true vine, and my Father is the vinegrower. He removes every branch in me that bears no fruit. Every branch that bears fruit he prunes to make it bear more fruit. You have already been cleansed by the word that I have spoken to you. Abide in me as I abide in you. Just as the branch cannot bear fruit by itself unless it abides in the vine, neither can you unless you abide in me. I am the vine, you are the branches. Those who abide in me and I in them bear much fruit, because apart from me you can do nothing. Whoever does not abide in me is thrown away like a branch and withers; such branches are gathered, thrown into the fire, and burned. If you abide in me, and my words abide in you, ask for whatever you wish, and it will be done for you. My Father is glorified by this, that you bear much fruit and become my disciples."

Year C

John 13:31-35

At the last supper, when Judas had gone out, Jesus said, "Now the Son of Man has been glorified, and God has been glorified in him. If God has been glorified in him, God will also glorify him in himself and will glorify him at once. Little children, I am with you only a little longer. You will look for me; and as I said to the Jews so now I say to you, 'Where I am going, you cannot come.' I give you a new commandment, that you love one another. Just as I have loved you, you also should love one another. By this everyone will know that you are my disciples, if you have love for one another."

As we grapple with John 14:6, it was Simone Weil (1909-1943) who famously suggested that given a choice between Christ and the truth, you should pick the truth because then you end up falling into the arms of Christ. This is the extended location of this famous sentiment.

There was a young English Catholic there from whom I gained my first idea of the supernatural power of the sacraments because of the truly angelic radiance with which he seemed to be clothed after going to communion. Chance—for I always prefer saying chance rather than Providence—made of him a messenger to me. For he told me of the existence of those English poets of the seventeenth century who are named metaphysical. In reading them later on, I discovered the poem of which I read you what is unfortunately a very inadequate translation. It is called "Love." I learned it by heart. Often, at the culminating point of a violent headache, I make myself say it over, concentrating all my attention upon it and clinging with all my soul to the tenderness it enshrines. I used to think I was merely reciting it as a beautiful poem, but without my knowing it the recitation had the virtue of a prayer. It was during one of these recitations that, as I told you, Christ himself came down and took possession of me.

In my arguments about the insolubility of the problem of God I had never foreseen the possibility of that, of a real contact, person to person, here below, between a human being and God. I had vaguely heard tell of things of this kind, but I had never believed in them. In the Fioretti the accounts of apparitions rather put me off if anything, like the miracles in the Gospel. Moreover, in this sudden possession of me by Christ, neither my senses nor my imagination had any part; I only felt in the midst of my suffering the presence of a love, like that which one can read in the smile on a beloved face.

I had never read any mystical works because I had never felt any call to read them. In reading as in other things I have always striven to practice obedience. There is nothing more favorable to intellectual progress, for as far as possible I only read what I am hungry for at the moment when I have an appetite for it, and then I do not read, I eat. God in his mercy had prevented me from reading the mystics, so that it should be evident to me that I had not invented this absolutely unexpected contact.

Yet I still half refused, not my love but my intelligence. For it seemed to me certain, and I still think so today, that one can never wrestle enough with God if one does so out of pure regard for the truth. Christ likes us to prefer truth to him because, before being Christ, he is truth. If one turns aside from him to go toward the truth, one will not go far before falling into his arms.

After this I came to feel that Plato was a mystic, that all the Iliad is bathed in Christian light, and that Dionysus and Osiris are in a certain sense Christ himself; and my love was thereby redoubled.

I never wondered whether Jesus was or was not the Incarnation of God; but in fact I was incapable of thinking of him without thinking of him as God.

This Wendell Berry (b. 1934) poem, "Manifesto: The Mad Farmer Liberation Front," is a campaign for a mad farmer. With the gospel inviting us to encounter a "Jesus as Farmer," we are invited to connect the human stewardship of the soil and land.

Love the quick profit, the annual raise,
vacation with pay. Want more
of everything ready-made. Be afraid
to know your neighbors and to die.

And you will have a window in your head.
Not even your future will be a mystery
any more. Your mind will be punched in a card
and shut away in a little drawer.

When they want you to buy something
they will call you. When they want you
to die for profit they will let you know.
So, friends, every day do something
that won't compute. Love the Lord.
Love the world. Work for nothing.
Take all that you have and be poor.
Love someone who does not deserve it.

Denounce the government and embrace
the flag. Hope to live in that free
republic for which it stands.
Give your approval to all you cannot
understand. Praise ignorance, for what man
has not encountered he has not destroyed.

Ask the questions that have no answers.
Invest in the millennium. Plant sequoias.
Say that your main crop is the forest

that you did not plant,
that you will not live to harvest.

Say that the leaves are harvested
when they have rotted into the mold.
Call that profit. Prophesy such returns.
Put your faith in the two inches of humus
that will build under the trees
every thousand years.

Listen to carrion—put your ear
close, and hear the faint chattering
of the songs that are to come.
Expect the end of the world. Laugh.
Laughter is immeasurable. Be joyful
though you have considered all the facts.
So long as women do not go cheap
for power, please women more than men.

Ask yourself: Will this satisfy
a woman satisfied to bear a child?
Will this disturb the sleep
of a woman near to giving birth?

Go with your love to the fields.
Lie down in the shade. Rest your head
in her lap. Swear allegiance
to what is nighest your thoughts.

As soon as the generals and the politicos
can predict the motions of your mind,
lose it. Leave it as a sign
to mark the false trail, the way
you didn't go.

Be like the fox
who makes more tracks than necessary,
some in the wrong direction.
Practice resurrection.

The glorification of the Son is linked with the obligation to love one another. St. John of the Cross, the famous Spanish mystic (1542-1591) provides this profound meditation on the nature of grace. It is called "What is Grace?"

"What is grace?" I asked God.
And He said,
"All that happens."
Then He added, when I looked perplexed,
"Could not lovers
say that every moment in their Beloved's arms
was grace?
Existence is my arms,
though I well understand how one can turn
away from
me
until the heart has
Wisdom."

Translation by Daniel Ladinsky

The film *Sideways* (2004) is ostensibly the story of two men named Miles and Jack who are coming to grips with mid-life crises—one is about to be married, the other is trying to make sense of his life and struggling career as an author. On their wine-tasting journey in Santa Barbara, they meet two local women, who match them in wine enthusiasm and seasoned wisdom. One of the women, a waitress named Maya, proves her mettle to Miles when she gives him a soliloquy about the appreciation of wine and the care that went into harvesting the grapes on the vine.

THE SIXTH SUNDAY
OF EASTER

Year A

John 14:15-21

Jesus said, "If you love me, you will keep my commandments. And I will ask the Father, and he will give you another Advocate, to be with you forever. This is the Spirit of truth, whom the world cannot receive, because it neither sees him nor knows him. You know him, because he abides with you, and he will be in you. "I will not leave you orphaned; I am coming to you. In a little while the world will no longer see me, but you will see me; because I live, you also will live. On that day you will know that I am in my Father, and you in me, and I in you. They who have my commandments and keep them are those who love me; and those who love me will be loved by my Father, and I will love them and reveal myself to them."

Year B

John 15:9-17

Jesus said to his disciples, "As the Father has loved me, so I have loved you; abide in my love. If you keep my commandments, you will abide in my love, just as I have kept my Father's commandments and abide in his love. I have said these things to you so that my joy may be in you, and that your joy may be complete. "This is my commandment, that you love one another as I have loved you. No one has greater love than this, to lay down one's life for one's friends. You are my friends if you do what I command you. I do not call you servants any longer, because the servant does not know what the master is doing; but I have called you friends, because I have made known to you everything that I have heard from my Father. You did not choose me but I chose you. And I appointed you to go and bear fruit, fruit that will last, so that the Father will give you whatever you ask him in my name. I am giving you these commands so that you may love one another."

Year C

John 14:23-29

Jesus said to Judas (not Iscariot), "Those who love me will keep my word, and my Father will love them, and we will come to them and make our home with them. Whoever does not love me does not keep my words; and the word that you hear is not mine, but is from the Father who sent me. "I have said these things to you while I am still with you. But the Advocate, the Holy Spirit, whom the Father will send in my name, will teach you everything, and remind you of all that I have said to you. Peace I leave with you; my peace I give to you. I do not give to you as the world gives. Do not let your hearts be troubled, and do not let them be afraid. You heard me say to you, 'I am going away, and I am coming to you.' If you loved me, you would rejoice that I am going to the Father, because the Father is greater than I. And now I have told you this before it occurs, so that when it does occur, you may believe."

Jesus promises to ask the Father to send the disciples another Advocate. In 1945, the Rodgers and Hammerstein musical *Carousel* introduced the world to this famous song, "You'll Never Walk Alone," which has since become the anthem of Liverpool Football Club. Nettie sings the song to comfort her friend Julie after her husband dies. When we "walk through a storm"—with all the fear and lack of hope, the invitation is to "walk on with hope" in our hearts. The author of John has Jesus in this Farewell Discourse preparing disciples for his departure. The invitation here is that the disciples should "never walk alone."

This moving poem "At a Calvary* Near the Ancre," was probably written towards the end of 1917 or at the beginning of 1918. Wilfred Owen (1893-1918) takes the image of the soldiers keeping watch at the cross and applies this to the situation he was facing as a soldier involved in fighting at the river Ancre. He invites the reader to see the tension between patriotism and faith. Towards the end of the poem, Owen explicitly alludes to this gospel and the sacrifice of the soldier who lays down his life for his friends.

One ever hangs where shelled roads part.
In this war He too lost a limb,
But His disciples hide apart;
And now the Soldiers bear with Him.
Near Golgotha strolls many a priest,
And in their faces there is pride
That they were flesh-marked by the Beast
By whom the gentle Christ's denied.
The scribes on all the people shove
And bawl allegiance to the state,
But they who love the greater love
Lay down their life; they do not hate.

A "Calvary" is a statue of the crucified Christ; these crucifixes are erected at many crossroads in France.

In John 14: 23-29 Jesus reveals as he talks with Judas (not Iscariot, but perhaps the son of James) that he is not interested in hiding knowledge. Jesus foretells his Ascension and that he will go to the Father. His message is love and peace, not regret or a call for repentance. Jesus is going to God the Father who is the everlasting source of love and peace, even the being of love and peace. An ancient prayer from the Syrian Clementine liturgy reveals God's nature and our relationship to the Father through the Son.

> O God, you are the unsearchable abyss of peace, the ineffable sea of love, the fountain of blessings and the bestower of affection, who sends peace to those who receive it. Open to us this day the sea of your love and water us with abundant streams from the riches of your grace and from the most sweet springs of your kindness. Make us children of quietness and heirs of peace; enkindle in us the fire of your love; sow in us your fear; strengthen our weakness by your power; bind us closely to you and to each other in our firm and indissoluble bond of unity.

In John 15, Jesus gives us the new commandment. One of the most powerful pieces of writing about love and listening comes from *Count It All Joy* by William Stringfellow (1928-1985), who was an American theologian and activist. His actual discussion comes in the context of listening to scripture with appropriate sensitivity to the text, but it has a broader application to the nature of love.

> Listening is a rare happening among human beings. You cannot listen to the word another is speaking if you are preoccupied with your appearance or impressing the other, or if you are trying to decide what you are going to say when the other stops talking, or if you are debating about whether the word being spoken is true or relevant or agreeable. Such matters may have their place, but only after listening to the word as the word is being uttered. Listening, in other words, is a primitive act of love, in which a person gives self to another's word, making self accessible and vulnerable to that word.

ASCENSION DAY

Year A, B, and C

Luke 24:44-53

Jesus said to his disciples, "These are my words that I spoke to you while I was still with you—that everything written about me in the law of Moses, the prophets, and the psalms must be fulfilled." Then he opened their minds to understand the scriptures, and he said to them, "Thus it is written, that the Messiah is to suffer and to rise from the dead on the third day, and that repentance and forgiveness of sins is to be proclaimed in his name to all nations, beginning from Jerusalem. You are witnesses of these things. And see, I am sending upon you what my Father promised; so stay here in the city until you have been clothed with power from on high." Then he led them out as far as Bethany, and, lifting up his hands, he blessed them. While he was blessing them, he withdrew from them and was carried up into heaven. And they worshiped him, and returned to Jerusalem with great joy; and they were continually in the temple blessing God.

James Baldwin (1924-1987) was an African American poet, novelist, and social critic. His life was spent exploring the web of class distinctions, the sin of racism and the complexity of sexuality. Long before gay rights were front and center, Baldwin's second and acclaimed novel, *Giovanni's Room*, in 1956 gave America a window into the lives of gay and bisexual men who were longing for acceptance. In *Go Tell It on the Mountain*, Baldwin sees the heavenly city ascending as Jesus ascended. We wait for the Ascended Christ as God waits for us.

Then John saw the river, and the multitude was there. And now they had undergone a change; their robes were ragged, and stained with the road they had traveled, and stained with unholy blood; the robes of some barely covered their nakedness; and some indeed were naked. And some stumbled on the smooth stones at the river's edge, for they were blind; and some crawled with a terrible wailing, for they were lame; some did not cease to pluck at their flesh, which was rotten with running sores. All struggled to get to the river, in a dreadful hardness of heart: the strong struck down the weak, the ragged spat on the naked, the naked cursed the blind, the blind crawled over the lame. And someone cried: "Sinner, do you love my Lord?"

Then John saw the Lord—for a moment only; and the darkness, for a moment only, was filled with a light he could not bear. Then, in a moment, he was set free; his tears sprang as from a fountain; his heart, like a fountain of waters, burst. Then he cried: 'Oh, blessed Jesus! Oh, Lord Jesus! Take me through!'

Of tears there was, yes, a very fountain—springing from a depth never sounded before, from depths John had not known were in him. And he wanted to rise up, singing, singing in that great morning, the morning of his new life. Ah, how his tears ran down, how they blessed his soul!—as he felt himself, out of the darkness, and the fire, and the terrors of death, rising upward to meet the saints. "Oh, yes!" cried the voice of Elisha. "Bless our God forever!"

And a sweetness filled John as he heard this voice, and heard the sound of singing: the singing was for him. For his drifting soul was anchored in the love of God; in the rock that endured for ever. The light and the darkness had kissed each other, and were married now, for ever, in the life and the vision of John's soul.

I, John, saw a city, way in the middle of the air,
Waiting, waiting, waiting up there.

Charles Williams (1886-1945) was a poet who was part of the Inklings, which included C.S. Lewis and J.R.R. Tolkien. For Williams, the Ascension was "then" and part of the first coming of Jesus. We now live in the "now" and the Church was forced to become "universal and durable" like time itself. It is the "Second Coming" that will mark the end of time and presumably the last transformation of the Church Universal.

Excerpt from The Descent of the Dove

The Church expected the Second Coming of Christ immediately, and no doubt this was so in the ordinary literal sense. But it was certainly expected also in another sense. The converts in all the cities of Asia and (soon) of Europe where the small groups were founded had known, in their conversion, one way or another, a first coming of their Redeemer. And then? And then! That was the consequent task and trouble—the then. He had come, and they adored and believed, they communicated and practiced, and waited for his further exhibition of himself. The then lasted, and there seemed to be no farther equivalent Now. Time became the individual and catholic problem. The Church had to become as catholic—as universal and as durable—as time.

The "heavenly" nanny Mary Poppins (Julie Andrews) successfully brings the Banks family back together through the course of the musical *Mary Poppins* (1964). All that is left for her to do is return to the clouds, when the wind changes direction once again. The film concludes with Mary rising back skyward while the family frolics together in the park, having been changed for the better, thanks to her.

Jesus went with his disciples as far as Bethany. He lifted up his hands, blessed them and then was "carried" into heaven. This last "act" in the drama of Jesus's earthly ministry is hard to grasp. There have been many attempts to explain the transport of Jesus into heaven itself. How was Jesus carried? Who carried him? Led Zeppelin's "Stairway to Heaven" is a profound meditation on "ignorant materialism;" the idea that we could, out of human achievements, build a way to heaven. Jesus is received into heaven because of his obedience to the Father: this is the truth about Jesus's ascent into heaven.

THE SEVENTH SUNDAY
OF EASTER

Year A

John 17:1-11

Jesus looked up to heaven and said, "Father, the hour has come; glorify your Son so that the Son may glorify you, since you have given him authority over all people, to give eternal life to all whom you have given him. And this is eternal life, that they may know you, the only true God, and Jesus Christ whom you have sent. I glorified you on earth by finishing the work that you gave me to do. So now, Father, glorify me in your own presence with the glory that I had in your presence before the world existed. I have made your name known to those whom you gave me from the world. They were yours, and you gave them to me, and they have kept your word. Now they know that everything you have given me is from you; for the words that you gave to me I have given to them, and they have received them and know in truth that I came from you; and they have believed that you sent me. I am asking on their behalf; I am not asking on behalf of the world, but on behalf of those whom you gave me, because they are yours. All mine are yours, and yours are mine; and I have been glorified in them. And now I am no longer in the world, but they are in the world, and I am coming to you. Holy Father, protect them in your name that you have given me, so that they may be one, as we are one."

Year B

John 17:6-19

Jesus prayed for his disciples, "I have made your name known to those whom you gave me from the world. They were yours, and you gave them to me, and they have kept your word. Now they know that everything you have given me is from you; for the words that you gave to me I have given to them, and they have received them and know in truth that I came from you; and they have believed that you sent me. I am asking on their behalf; I am not asking on behalf of the world, but on behalf of those whom you gave me, because they are yours. All mine are yours, and yours are mine; and I have been glorified in them. And now I am no longer in the world, but they are in the world, and I am coming to you. Holy Father, protect them in your name that you have given me, so that they may be one, as we are one. While I was with them, I protected them in your name that you have given me. I guarded them, and not one of them was lost except the one destined to be lost, so that the scripture might be fulfilled. But now I am coming to you, and I speak these things in the world so that they may have my joy made complete in themselves. I have given them your word, and the world has hated them because they do not belong to the world, just as I do not belong to the world. I am not asking you to take them out of the world, but I ask you to protect them from the evil one. They do not belong to the world, just as I do not belong to the world. Sanctify them in the truth; your word is truth. As you have sent me into the world, so I have sent them into the world. And for their sakes I sanctify myself, so that they also may be sanctified in truth."

Year C

John 17:20-26

Jesus prayed for his disciples, and then he said. "I ask not only on behalf of these, but also on behalf of those who will believe in me through their word, that they may all be one. As you, Father, are in me and I am in you, may they also be in us, so that the world may believe that you have sent me. The glory that you have given me I have given them, so that they may be one, as we are one, I in them and you in me, that they may become completely one, so that the world may know that you have sent me and have loved them even as you have loved me. Father, I desire that those also, whom you have given me, may be with me where I am, to see my glory, which you have given me because you loved me before the foundation of the world. Righteous Father, the world does not know you, but I know you; and these know that you have sent me. I made your name known to them, and I will make it known, so that the love with which you have loved me may be in them, and I in them."

As Jesus anticipates his death, Jesus is worried about his disciples. W.H. Auden (1907-1973), the unsurpassed Anglo-American poet, was the chancellor of the Academy of American Poets from 1954 to 1973. This craggy-faced poet, who lived between New York City and Vienna, is known for his love poems and for epics such as *For the Time Being*. He was concerned about the human condition and the spiritual forces which shaped the "age of anxiety," which was very much his age and the age of those who influenced him, such as T.S. Eliot, Marx, and Freud.

> We would rather be ruined than changed
> We would rather die in our dread
> Than climb the cross of the moment
> And let our illusions die.

Emily Dickinson, the nineteenth-century American poet, was greatly influenced by the Reverend Charles Wadsworth on a trip to Philadelphia. Most of her life, however, was lived in virtual isolation from the outside world. Hers was a Calvinist, orthodox, and conservative approach to Christianity, influenced by the Metaphysical poets of seventeenth-century England and also a reading of the Book of Revelation—all in a Puritan New England town. In many ways, Dickinson lived the prayer which Jesus said with his disciples in John 17.

> This World is not conclusion.
> A Species stands beyond—
> Invisible, as Music—
> But positive, as Sound—
> It beckons, and it baffles—
> Philosophy, don't know—
> And through a Riddle, at the last—
> Sagacity, must go—
> To guess it, puzzles scholars—
> To gain it, Men have borne
> Contempt of Generations
> And Crucifixion, shown—
> Faith slips—and laughs, and rallies—
> Blushes, if any see—
> Plucks at a twig of Evidence—
> And asks a Vane, the way—
> Much Gesture, from the Pulpit—
> Strong Hallelujahs roll—
> Narcotics cannot still the Tooth
> That nibbles at the soul—

The prayer for Christian unity looks like a prayer that was unanswered. In these gospel lessons, Jesus affirms the efficacy of prayer. Did Jesus pray because he needed to? Were all Jesus's prayers answered? Richard Hooker (1554-1600), Anglican Divine and apologist of the Elizabethan Settlement of 1559, wrote of Jesus's last prayer and wrestled with its meaning, its implications. Did Jesus need to give thanks?

> That Christ, as the only begotten Son of God, having no superior, and therefore owing honour unto none, neither standing in any need, should either give thanks, or make petition unto God, were most absurd. As man what could beseem him better, whether we respect his affection to Godward, or his own necessity, or his charity and love towards men? Some things he knew should come to pass and notwithstanding prayed for them, because he also knew that the necessary means to effect them were his prayers. As in the Psalm it is said, "Ask of me and I will give thee the heathen for thine inheritance and the ends of the earth for thy possession." Wherefore that which here God promiseth his Son, the same in the seventeenth of John he prayeth for: "Father, the hour is now come, glorify thy Son, that thy Son also may glorify thee according as thou hast given him power over all flesh."
>
> But had Christ the like promise concerning the effect of every particular for which he prayed? That which was not effected could not be promised. And we know in what sort he prayed for removal of that bitter cup, which cup he tasted, notwithstanding his prayer.

In the seventeenth chapter of John, our Lord's farewell prayer is addressed to God the Father. When Jesus speaks in verse 17:19 of "sanctifying Himself," we realize the primary emphasis is not ethics but holiness. Susanna Hopton (1627-1709), a devotional writer who knew the seventeenth-century Anglican Divines, wrote "On our Saviour's Prayer John 17":

> After all the foregoing Precepts of Holiness, and Promises of Mercy and Comforts, which thou, O blessed Jesus, didst give into thy Disciples, and in them to all thine, what a Prayer of Zeal, Love, Care, Wisdom, Power, and Efficacy, didst thou make for thy self, for thine Apostles, Disciples, and all thine, lifting up thine eyes to Heaven, and praying for thine own Glory, saying, Father glorify thy Son, that thy Son also may glorify thee: As thou hast given him Power over all Flesh, that he should give eternal Life to as many as thou hast given him: And this is life eternal to know thee, the only true God, and Jesus Christ whom thou has sent:
>
> I praise and magnify thy Name.
>
> And I beseech thee lift up mine Heart and Eyes unto thee, and thou who knowest what eternal Life is, shew a Glympse thereof unto me. For I see the Knowledge of God is eternal Life, O grant that Knowledge to me. Amen.